POETS AND SAINTS

"Jamie George is one of our generation's most inspired storytellers. He not only is able to bring a story to life, but he plants you right in the middle of it. In *Poets and Saints*, you will find yourself in a secret English garden, sharing a pint at the Eagle and Child in Oxford, standing in the shadows of Notre-Dame, and awestruck on a hillside in Assisi. You will meet a cast of unlikely characters and the stories they uncover. It was not only a privilege to take this journey with my friend and pastor, but it was a privilege to read his words and be reminded that God has woven the past and present together in a remarkable and vibrant way."

Leslie Jordan, All Sons & Daughters

"Jamie has truly captured the voices and hearts of these extremely special individuals. The stories revealed on these pages will inspire, challenge, and spark creativity. I feel honored to have been a part of this adventure, and I know you will feel the same as you read this."

David Leonard, All Sons & Daughters

"I've always said that the best teachers are storytellers, and Jamie George is one of the best storytellers I know. I've been blessed by hearing him tell his stories in person for years. Now it's your turn!"

Dave Ramsey, *New York Times* bestselling author
and nationally syndicated radio show host

"Jamie cuts through the religious stereotypes. His laid-back, transparent style of storytelling is extremely refreshing and encouraging for a guy like me, who was raised in the church and feels like he has seen it all. Jamie is a new friend that we all truly need to hear from."

Jeremy Cowart, photographer and
founder of Help-Portrait

"Jamie George is a masterful storyteller with a penchant for real-life situational significance. I've never felt comfortable with church or its confines, but I am proud to call Jamie my pastor, friend, and fellow artist."

Kevin Max, artist and author, formally
with DC Talk & Audio Adrenaline

POETS & SAINTS

Eternal Insight. Extravagant Love.
Ordinary People.

POETS & SAINTS

JAMIE GEORGE

David C Cook
transforming lives together

POETS AND SAINTS
Published by David C Cook
4050 Lee Vance View
Colorado Springs, CO 80918 U.S.A.

David C Cook U.K., Kingsway Communications
Eastbourne, East Sussex BN23 6NT, England

The graphic circle C logo is a registered trademark of David C Cook.

The website addresses recommended throughout this book are offered as a
resource to you. These websites are not intended in any way to be or imply an
endorsement on the part of David C Cook, nor do we vouch for their content.

LCCN 2016939760
Hardcover ISBN 978-1-4347-1125-0
Paperback Edition ISBN 978-1-4347-0998-1
eISBN 978-0-7814-1444-9

The Team: Alice Crider, Amy Konyndyk, Nick Lee, Jennifer
Lonas, Helen Macdonald, Susan Murdock
Cover Design: Joe Cavazos Design
Cover Photo: Zach Prichard

Printed in the United States of America
First Edition 2016

2 3 4 5 6 7 8 9 10

080516-LS

To the Journey Church—
You are poets and saints for the ages, and I will never
forget you. I have a feeling the world won't either.

CONTENTS

ACKNOWLEDGMENTS

My wife, Angie—for your steadfast belief in me and us.

My son Jordan—for your pursuit of God and your artistic expression.

My son Tyler—for your teachable spirit and passion for truth.

My daughter Ashton—for your compassion and creativity.

My daughter Addison—for your laughter, hugs, and "I love yous."

Leslie Jordan—for your friendship, your incessant pursuit of truth, and your willingness to share your inspiration.

David Leonard—for your friendship, your kindness, and your willingness to share your extraordinary talent.

My parents, sisters, brothers-in-law, nephews, and nieces—each of you has a song to sing and a place in my heart.

My wife's family, the McIntyres and Shirleys—for your love and support.

Terri Perkins—for your generosity; this book was born in a stable.

Verne Kenney—for believing.

Esther Fedorkevich—you are a hurricane of goodwill toward men.

Amy Gregory Spence—your hammering on the anvil continues to form me.

Chris DeTray—you and Jesus hold all things together.

Sarah MacIntosh—your insightful delivery is ever delightful.

Zach Prichard—for your enthusiasm for life and stunning visual artistry.

Thomas Jordan, Natalie Leonard, and Brea DeTray—for your trust.

Cara Fox and Matt Underwood—for your respective artistic prowess.

Randy and Katie Williams—for your faithfulness and generous love.

Paul Farmer—for your X-ray vision and ceaseless encouragement.

Michael Smallbone—for your warrior spirit of protection and truth.

ACKNOWLEDGMENTS

Nick Barre—for your insight about insight.

Joel Smallbone—for being a friend in the truest sense of that word.

Aaron Nebrija—for sharing the load and the dream.

Kevin Dixon—for your nonchalant rescue and confident shrugs.

Laurie Lokey—for your guiding hand and tender heart.

Alice Crider—for your steadfast confidence and collaborative spirit.

Tim Close—for telling the story of the story.

Darren Whitehead—for providing a home for the homeless.

Jacqui Dakin—for keeping the compass heading true north.

Terry and Susie Dunham—for hugs and bookshelves.

PREVIEW

I spent a lot of time alone as a child. My friend Laurie, a therapist, tells me it's probably because when I was alone, I didn't feel the pressure to rescue people. She's probably right, because when I was alone, I drew pictures of me rescuing people.

When I wasn't drawing, I was reading books about history. And stories about people who needed rescuing.

I've spent the past decade learning what it means to serve people and lead them to the Messiah, rather than trying to be one.

Now when I read history, I glance backward through a different lens. I'm drawn to men and women who seemed to achieve a confidence in their roles as co-conspirators in the mission of God. Men and women content to allow the Father to govern, His Son to save, and His Spirit to guide.

These unusual people were formed into conduits of God's love, and over the course of time, His followers have labeled them: poets and saints.

Poets and saints have inspired us with their books, their poems, their songs, the way they loved, and the way they lived. They must not be forgotten. Their words have stood the test of time and are as important for us today as they were for their contemporaries. Found in their insights are nuggets of truth that through the years have been forged into bonds of iron among the people of God. When we debate with dignity and agree with love, we hold together those sacred convictions that set us apart and cut a path for the return of the King.

Though the Christian community has called some men and women saints, it's not because they were perfect. It's because we remember them for the way they lived out their faith. They were not without their issues. They were as messed up as you and I. And this gives me hope. If God can use the brokenness and suffering of these Christian icons, He can do the same for me.

I pastor a church filled with wanderers and misfits, artists and adventurers. We're a motley crew who have signed up for apprenticeship in the Jesus way. We vacillate in our hopes and fears but press on, trusting in the ability of our master.

Our inspiration comes from the past.

Our hope lies in the future.

Our perspiration is in the present.

We have little idea what's next, but we are willing servants stepping out in faith.

                  .

I get to do this as a pastor. As a husband. And as a father. Recognizing that trials and tests produce perseverance, I concocted a rite-of-passage experience for my children. After having some success hiking along the Appalachian Trail during a heat wave with my twin sons when they were sixteen, I decided it was time to craft a challenging adventure for my sixteen-year-old daughter, Ashton.

For a child who longs to travel, loves to organize, and dislikes unplanned interruptions, a trip across the Pond seemed like just the thing.

I announced to Ashton, "I'm taking you to Europe!"

She hugged me and began planning.

Soon after, while I was discussing our church-history series with our church's creative-arts team, wonderful ideas began intersecting.

Within a few weeks our worship band All Sons & Daughters—including leaders Leslie Jordan and David Leonard and manager Chris DeTray—and my literary agent, Esther Fedorkevich, collaborated and then proposed an idea to our publisher.

What if Leslie, David, and I filmed a two-week documentary-style study for churches that taught church history in an engaging way, featuring icons of the faith from Europe?

And what if the band wrote songs from their experiences retracing the steps of these European poets and saints? And what if I recorded our experiences in a book that combined snapshots of biographical information fused with teaching on spiritual formation? The publisher said it sounded crazy ... and then said yes.

So David, Leslie, and I went about gathering the team.

David and his wife, Natalie.

Leslie and her husband, Thomas.

Chris and his wife, Brea.

Sarah MacIntosh, recording artist and researcher.

Cara Fox, cellist.

Zach Prichard, film director.

Matt Underwood, cameraman.

Jordan and Tyler George, artists and crew (who joined us halfway through the trip).

And Ashton and me.

Feeling energized as the plan unfolded, I introduced it to Ashton: "We have a new opportunity. I'm still taking you to Europe for your rite-of-passage experience, but how would you feel about also functioning as my assistant on a project with my publisher? This way we can save a little money and visit a few more sites than we would have otherwise been able to. You'll ride on a sleeper bus with eleven other people, and you'll be able to see Paris."

"What's the trade-off?" she asked, processing what might be lost in the new arrangement.

"Less time with your dad."

She paused for a moment. "Did you say Paris?! When do we leave?"

Ashton wasn't the only one excited to see Europe. While my twin sons, Jordan and Tyler, and I had dreamed of backpacking around the continent after they graduated high school, they now had a new motivation. My boys are musicians who made their first splash on YouTube and have since gathered an international fan base. By tagging along, they would get to connect with their European fans. The boys planned to fly to Paris the same morning Ashton would be traveling back to the States. And when the team flew home, my sons and I would rent a car and rough it on our own for a couple more weeks.

So it was with great anticipation that the trip of a lifetime was set in motion. There was so much to learn. And learn we did.

From a pub in Oxford, England, to a basilica nestled high in the Italian hills to a rooftop in Switzerland where the coals of the Reformation were stoked, our team traveled across the European continent, wondering what we might learn about the history of our faith.

In the end we discovered much more than facts, figures, and biographies.

We found faith itself. In the people of God. Poets and saints. Crazy thing was, they weren't all dead. Some of them were sleeping in the bunk next to us. And there's a pretty good chance one of them is holding this book.

Chapter 1

MAY LOVE FIND US

Saint Patrick, AD 387–461, Ireland

You hold it all together.

"You Hold It All Together," All Sons & Daughters

As we flew over the Atlantic Ocean toward Dublin, Ireland, Ashton and I shifted uncomfortably in our seats, trying to get some much-needed shut-eye. It was my daughter's sixteenth birthday and also marked day one of her rite-of-passage experience.

I finally dozed off two hours before we were scheduled to land but was abruptly awakened when Ashton jerked violently next to me. To my horror, she looked as white as a ghost, her eyelids fluttering about wildly. She was fading in and out of consciousness.

Panicked, I grabbed her face and shouted, "Ashton! Ashton! Wake up! Look at me!" No response. Only grunting sounds emanated from her throat. Unsure of what to do, I pushed the service call button, and a flight attendant came quickly to our seats.

"My daughter is on the verge of passing out!" I exclaimed. "Can you help me?"

Springing into action, the concerned attendant helped me get Ashton out of her seat and into the service area at the center of the plane. We laid her down and propped up her legs while another helpful flight attendant placed an oxygen mask over Ashton's face.

A few minutes later, a young man walked up and introduced himself as a doctor. "Something is seriously wrong with my daughter," I blurted out. He offered to help and began rattling off a series of questions. Taking Ashton's blood pressure, which was unusually low, he asked how much water she'd had that day. I wasn't sure. Then it hit me.

In a show of solidarity, and because at the ripe old age of forty-five I knew it would be good for me, Ashton and I had engaged in a hard-core exercise and nutrition plan before our trip. We celebrated her birthday (and the end of our restricted eating) by spending the day at the pool and indulging in cake and ice cream. After twenty-one days of drinking half our bodies' weight in water, this was the first day we had ignored our disciplines. I figured Ashton had consumed a glass of water at most and relayed this to the doc. Dr. Jon nodded confidently, concluding that she was dehydrated. He explained that being on an airplane accentuates the symptoms of dehydration, causing blood pressure to drop and potentially resulting in a loss of consciousness.

For the next two hours, Dr. Jon, my new favorite person on the planet, and I closely monitored a fatigued Ashton while she sipped juice and water. Toward the end of our flight, she seemed to be getting better. When the wheels touched down, and after lavishing gratitude on the good doctor and the Irish flight attendants, my daughter and I walked off the plane to a waiting wheelchair on the Jetway. There a cheery, young Irish woman accompanied us on our passage through customs.

While our final destination was London, where we had arranged to meet the band and our production team, the nine-hour layover in Dublin afforded Ashton and me some time to explore the city.

To my relief, by this time Ashton was now mostly revived. Sitting on a bus as it lurched through the streets of the Irish capital, I turned to my daughter and let out a sigh. "Wow," I said, smiling. "I wanted your rite of passage to be difficult, but I wasn't expecting it to start quite this way."

THE BIRTH OF CHRISTIANITY

After scarfing down replenishing burgers and chips at Bóbós, a favorite local eatery, and with plenty of time to visit a couple of the historic sites in Dublin, Ashton and I headed toward the first destination on our list: Saint Patrick's Cathedral.

I had recently become fascinated with Saint Patrick and was looking forward to exploring the grand cathedral that bears his name. Though Patrick is one of the more popular Catholic saints and has a color-themed holiday in his honor in the United States, many Americans have little idea how his life influenced the spiritual trajectory of the world.

To understand Patrick's story, it's helpful to know the backdrop.

Around AD 33–35, the explosive beginnings of Christianity occurred at the cross section of three dominant cultures: Hebrew, Greek, and Roman. Emboldened by the resurrection, Jesus' early disciples began teaching and preaching the gospel, the dynamic, mind-blowing news that God loved the human race so much that He offered a sacrifice, His only child, to redeem the world. Like a lamb to the slaughter, this Son of God died for the sins of humankind, and three days later came back to life. World religion at the time was full of myths and parables, but this was the first God to visit the planet as a human and then die on behalf of its people, His creation.

This news spread like wildfire. The world was being introduced to a kind, just, and trustworthy God who clothed Himself in flesh and walked among us. And by the thousands, people believed.

As the first few centuries passed, the church experienced major transitions. The most significant was the shift from being a persecuted faith (the Roman government regularly tortured followers of Jesus by burning them alive or feeding them to lions) to, in just a few hundred years, the Roman Empire's official religion. Once existing on the margins of society as an outcast faith, Christianity was embraced as the central pillar of religious culture. By AD 380, people were persecuted for *not* being Christian. As we shall see in the lives of future saints, the institutionalization of the church presented a host of new challenges.

Benefiting from a common world language and the massive expansion of Roman roadways and shipping lanes, the church grew rapidly. While it made great strides in mainland Europe, little effort was employed to reaching people outside the civilized world, such as the Celts in Ireland. Some even believed there wasn't any point in sharing the good news with such barbaric tribes, since they were presumably not civilized enough to grasp it. This way of thinking has affected the church throughout its history, even up to the present. For instance, many still believe that other cultures must adopt particular styles of dress and language to be Christian. (Have you ever seen pictures of native African pastors wearing polyester suits in rural villages?)

Change took place in the fifth century by way of a young Briton with an interesting past. In time, history would remember this man as "the first missionary to barbarians beyond the reach of Roman law. The step he took was in its way as bold as Columbus's, and a thousand times more humane."[1]

PATRICK'S EARLY LIFE

Born in the late fourth century, Maewyn Succat (given the name Patrick years later at his ordination) grew up in Britain. His family was religious; his grandfather a priest. Throughout his early life, he likely memorized a catechism that afforded him a foundation in the biblical narrative. But from what we gather from historical records, Patrick and his prominent family experienced Christianity merely as an inherited social propriety, not as a passionate way of life.

At some point during Patrick's unruly teenage years, Celtic pirates from Ireland invaded his town. These lawless barbarians swept up the coast, capturing the young man and others in the melee. Although his parents and others escaped, Patrick was kidnapped, smuggled onto a pirate ship, and carried off to Ireland. He was eventually sold as a slave to a chieftain and taken two hundred miles inland. Cut off from everyone he had ever known, Patrick felt very alone.

Celtic culture was barbaric, with little sense of organization and civility and no centralized power. Instead, warring tribes battled for dominance, functioning a bit like cattle rustlers in the American West at the turn of the twentieth century.

As a slave, Patrick was tasked with the responsibilities of a shepherd, which isolated him even further. For weeks at a time, he moved sheep from pasture to pasture, his only company his woolly friends. In his brief memoir later published as *The Confession of Saint Patrick*, Patrick said the afflictions most overwhelming during this time were the freezing cold and the pain of hunger.

How did a teenager thrown into a cauldron of emotional and physical suffering handle the experience? Did he become bitter, disgruntled, or angry with God?

Quite the opposite.

We can imagine that the biblical narratives Patrick memorized as a child came to life in his mind and heart. As noted in his memoir, he began to pray hundreds of times a day.[2] Through this practice, he formed a connection with God that he hadn't previously experienced. He began to sense God's Spirit in powerful ways. Surrounded by creation—vast, green pastures; gentle, bleating sheep; the wisps of clouds that stretched across the azure sky—Patrick began to notice the splendor of the Creator.

He wrote, "The Lord opened up my awareness of my lack of faith. Even though it came about late, I recognised my failings. So I turned with all my heart to the Lord my God, and he looked down on my lowliness and had mercy on my youthful ignorance. He guarded me before I knew him, and before I came to wisdom and could distinguish between good and evil. He protected me and consoled me as a father does for his son."[3]

In this love exchange with God, even within the confines of slavery, Patrick was learning to be content and aware of the presence of the Divine. In his solitude Patrick found hope. In his hope he found Jesus. In Jesus he found a love that longed to be known.

Whether or not Patrick realized it, God was fashioning a certain rite of passage for him. The apathy of his early adolescence was transformed into awe and wonder for his heavenly Father.

Awe is an intuition for the dignity of all things.[4]

Abraham Joshua Heschel

Six years after his capture, Patrick was awakened from a deep sleep in the middle of the night. He heard the voice of God say, "Soon you will depart for your home country. Behold, your ship is ready."[5]

The next morning Patrick fled. As a runaway slave, he navigated his way unnoticed two hundred miles back to the sea. Arriving near an inlet, he trekked up and over the rise, and sure enough, a ship lay at anchor. The international merchants of that Roman vessel initially rejected him, but Patrick eventually negotiated his way on board and sailed back to the "continent." He was going home.

Imagine for a moment that you are Patrick, huddled deep in the hull of a ship, surrounded by strangers. Imagine your thoughts swaying back and forth with the foam-crested waves. Certainly the hope of freedom lies in front of you, but also present is a strange kind of grief. For in your sorrow and troubles, a song was birthed in your heart. It took slavery for your soul to be rescued.

Home awaits, but what kind of life will follow?

THE PRISONER RETURNS

Switch the role playing for a moment.

Imagine now that you're one of Patrick's parents, who has only partially grieved the loss of your kidnapped child. You have moments when, standing on the beach, looking out over the water, you cling to strands of hope that one day your son will return. But most days you live with the dull ache that tells you he's gone and you'll never look into his eyes again.

And then a knock.

You walk toward the door, wiping the work of the day on your apron. As you turn the knob and the door creaks open, a young man darkened by the sun and worn by the elements stands before you.

You know in an instant. Your heart flutters, and warmth floods your cheeks.

It's your son. He's alive. And he has come home.

I'm not sure how Patrick's mother responded that day. Perhaps she collapsed, cried, or praised God. And his dad? I wonder if he stood paralyzed in shock, or if he reached out and gripped his son the way a drowning man grips a life preserver.

I'm a parent. I know what it is to love a son. And I'm a son. I know what it is to love a parent. What a moment it must have been. From Tarzan to The Arrow, our culture is full of tales of this kind of death and rebirth. Patrick's story, however, was no myth. It was real. He was alive and much different from the boy who once played on the rocks nearby.

Patrick had been forever changed. He was no longer a Romano-Briton. Though he had grown up speaking Welsh and was schooled in classic

Latin, he spent many of his formative years in Ireland learning the Celtic ways and language. Radical extraction from his native culture followed by years of isolation made reentering his homeland an unnerving and painful experience. It's hard to know where you belong in a culture you no longer identify with.

Living in Nashville, I often minister to artists and entertainers. I've had long conversations with friends on the challenges of resuming life at home after weeks on the road. The wives of many musicians speak of their difficulty functioning like single mothers, only to have their routines interrupted when their husbands return home. Husbands share that after coming home, it sometimes takes days to reacclimate to a completely different rhythm of life. For both men and women, life is often fraught with conflict and disorientation as they navigate the nuances of time split between home and the road.

If this happens to folks spending short periods of time away from home, imagine the adjustment of a slave who suddenly became free. A displaced soul attempting to adapt to a former life.

The days and nights were difficult for Patrick.

While dozing off one evening, Patrick had a vision. In it he saw an Irishman holding up countless letters, one of them titled "The Voice of the Irish." When Patrick first saw these words, he heard the cries of the multitudes. In tears the Irish masses begged him to come back and walk among them once more.

When he awoke, Patrick was torn. He wrestled with what was clearly a call to return to the land of his former captors and carry to them the great hope of God's love. Though he no longer fit in back home in Britain, there was a reason he ran away from Ireland and its painful memories. Going back to the place of his enslavement wasn't quite what he had in mind.

Furthermore, Patrick carried with him a deep sense of shame from something that happened when he was fifteen years old. Some historians think Patrick may have killed someone, perhaps a maid or a servant. British society at the time was divided into a traditional social-class structure. The penalty for murder below your social class was minimal and was often overlooked. But while the government hadn't punished him for the crime, Patrick never forgot it. It remained a secret that weighed heavily upon him.

The vision recurred many times before Patrick finally responded to God. He said, in effect, *If this is from You, Lord, I am willing to go.*

Recognizing the need for ecclesiastical training, Patrick, it is surmised, moved to southern France, where he may have spent several years in a monastery learning spiritual practices and the ways of communal living. Some historians suggest that he later received formal theological training at a university in Auxerre. After Patrick had spent almost two decades acquiring the emotional and spiritual strength needed to return to Ireland, his superiors believed he was ready for a mission there and made preparations for his ordination to the priesthood.

As his ordination drew closer, Patrick couldn't shake the shame he felt from that unconfessed failure from his childhood. Finally he brought it to light, sharing it with church leadership and asking God for forgiveness. It seems it wasn't accidental that the one being called to a culture of violence understood the deep spiritual and emotional consequences of acting in a violent way. So at forty-eight years of age, Patrick was sent out as one of the first church planters to an unreached people group, the Celtic peoples of Ireland. And God, the redeemer of all things, empowered Patrick to pour out upon his captors the grace he had been shown.

Isn't it interesting that the failure we're most ashamed of is frequently the failure God chooses to use? As mentioned in the preview, I often succumb to the temptation to rescue people. In this way, I may prevent the tension and growth that the other person is meant to experience. Yet God in His grace chooses to reshape my brokenness for His glory, transforming my penchant to rescue others into a healthy empathy. Guided by His Spirit, I'm able to promote healing instead of absorbing pain.

What propensity or previous failure might God refashion for His purpose in your life?

LOVE MEETS PEOPLE WHERE THEY ARE

While certain leaders in the fourth-century church had specific strategies, methods, and purposes for evangelizing, we can speculate from his writings that Patrick had his own ideas. Unlike some of his contemporaries, it seems he had no interest in expanding the institutional church's power. Patrick's mission had a deeply relational tone. It appears that rather than dismissing the Irish culture, he engaged it. He connected with the Irish people by identifying their needs and initiating conversations about how those needs might be fulfilled in a Trinitarian God.

We can affirm the good instincts still present in surrounding culture while gently pointing to their source.[6]
Philip Yancey

This wasn't easy. According to his confession, after landing in Ireland, Patrick was continually placed in life-and-death situations. Characterized by unthrottled emotion, the tribal people threatened to torture and kill him. Many of the Irish were (and are) a fiery bunch. Their feelings could turn on a dime. This forced Patrick to trust God with his mortality. Despite the deadly perils he faced, this slave turned missionary continued to challenge the immorality of the Celtic way of life with a balance of confidence and love.

Ireland was a polytheistic society, and the people worshipped a number of mythical gods. Unlike the sculpted and refined Greek and Roman idols, Celtic deities looked monstrous, obscene, and profane. They were also known to be fickle tricksters. At any time and without warning, these gods could wreak havoc on the Irish, turning good luck into gross misfortune. This instilled great fear in the hearts of the people and, in turn, bred a fatalistic worldview. Because the Irish lived under such intense distress, courage was highly valued. In fact, given the dreadful masters they served, it was a necessity. Without it, one would have been unable to function in Celtic society. Likely, the people were impressed with Patrick's determination and courage. Such fearlessness demanded their attention.

It appears that Patrick would often engage the people by using their gods as a springboard for describing his God. Rather than rail against the Irish culture, he identified the truth within it.

Every religion is compelled to find a resolution for guilt and shame. Most religious followers understand that a sacrifice—something innocent—must be paid repeatedly to provide relief from these burdens. This is why child sacrifice was and still is prevalent in many societies. (Some argue that modern-day abortion is a sacrifice to the god of convenience.)

We get the impression from historians that while Patrick challenged the Celts, he didn't shame them for their misdeeds. It seems he acknowledged their understanding of the importance of sacrifice and used this common ground to introduce God the Father. In comparison to their three-headed gods,[7] it would have been natural for Patrick to explain how the Father—the first of the three faces—actually sacrificed His own Son, the second of the three faces. Patrick's message so captivated the Celts that he could then offer another revelation. He'd explain how the third face, the Holy Spirit, traded places with the second face and was active on the earth and even desired to empower them with a divine nature. He offered the people the good news that they could be freed from sin and shame and find purpose in following the triune God!

The blending of history and legend indicates that Patrick's patience, gentleness, kindness, and courage invited conversations that led to a sweeping spiritual renewal of the Irish people. In time they began to respond en masse to this message of salvation. They abandoned their pagan gods and followed Jesus.

> *This is the love of God: an alchemy that*
> *can turn enemies into children.*[8]
> Mark Buchanan

Patrick moved from clan to clan throughout the country, sharing the gospel and planting indigenous churches: "In becoming an Irishman, Patrick wedded his world to theirs, his faith to their life.... Patrick found a way of swimming down to the depths of the Irish psyche and warming and transforming Irish imagination—making it more humane and more noble while keeping it Irish."[9] Ireland is the only country in this era of history where mass conversion to Christianity happened without bloodshed.

THE GOSPEL REVEALED

In his book *The Celtic Way of Evangelism*, George G. Hunter offers an interesting contrast between the Roman and Patrician ways of expressing the gospel of Jesus Christ.[10] The Roman model includes three key markers, similar to the following script:

1. Presentation: Here is the message of salvation through Christ.

2. Decision: Would you like to make a decision to believe and accept this good news?

3. Fellowship: If so, welcome to the fold. If not, bummer for you.

According to this Roman way of evangelizing, everything hinges on a person's decision in the moment. If one decides not to believe the good news of God's love, the relationship comes to an end.

The Celtic, or Patrician, model is characterized this way:

1. Fellowship: I want to hear your story. Tell me about your culture. Tell me about your ways. I want to know you.

2. Ministry and conversation: I am well resourced because I believe in one God who has empowered me to serve you.

3. Invitation: If you will dedicate your life to this God, He will also indwell you and empower you to live a life much different from the one you've been living. Would you like to be a part of that story?

While there are obvious contrasts between the two approaches, one thing is certain: God uses different kinds of people with different kinds of methods to accomplish His purposes.

Billy Graham is a great example. There was a season in church history when God used evangelists in large public gatherings to present the gospel and then invite people to get out of their seats, walk down an aisle, and make an on-the-spot commitment to Jesus Christ. I was four or five years old when I watched this renowned evangelist on television for the first time. Curious, I asked my father why hundreds of people were pouring into the aisles of the large stadium.

"They want to follow Jesus," my dad replied.

I looked at him and said, "Well, I want to follow Jesus too." I climbed into my father's lap, feeling his arms wrap around me, and together we prayed. That day I told God I believed Jesus was His Son, and I wanted to give Him my life.

It's up for debate how much I could understand at the tender age of five and how many of those who gathered at the stadium stage that day actually followed Jesus. But it's difficult to refute that for a period in time, our culture responded to a Roman model of Christian evangelism.

Most of us understand that culture continually shifts. This is why it's important to question whether our ways of sharing the message of Jesus are still effective. How are we meant to interact with different cultures today? Are our methods of communicating competent?

And let's ask the tough question about power and control: In our expression of the good news, whose kingdom are we really interested in expanding?

Patrick allowed Celtic culture to breathe and morph with its newfound faith. He was less interested in expanding the Roman church and more interested in treating the Celts as image bearers of God. As such, he treated them as equals. His way was patient and subtle, and he allowed his listening to govern his talking. He modeled a way of love and then described Love's origins.

It would seem that Patrick spent time meditating on the following passage from the apostle Paul's letter to one of his church plants:

> Even though I am free of the demands and expectations of everyone, I have voluntarily become a servant to any and all in order to reach a wide range of people: religious, nonreligious, meticulous moralists, loose-living immoralists, the defeated, the demoralized—whoever. I didn't take on their way of life. I kept my bearings in Christ—but I entered their world and tried to experience things from their point of view. I've become just about every sort of servant there is in my attempts to lead those I meet into a God-saved life. I did all this because of the Message. I didn't just want to talk about it; I wanted to be in on it![11]

Patrick was deeply connected to the Irish people and their stories. He loved them. And he felt he had much to learn from them about himself. In his own words, "It was among foreigners that it was seen how little I was."[12]

If deep down you think you're a big deal, spend time with a group of people who don't understand you. You'll quickly learn how little you are and how big the world is.

SAINT PATRICK'S DAY

The first Saint Patrick's Day parade on March 17, 1762, took place not in Ireland but in New York City. It was meant to commemorate Patrick's legacy of bringing Christianity to the people of Ireland and their transformation through the love of God. This isn't what most people in our country associate with Saint Patrick's Day, however. (I once asked a crowd of about nine hundred people how many of them spent time on this holiday reflecting on and celebrating the Irish converting to Christianity. Only one hand raised.)

To put this lack of knowledge into perspective, it's the equivalent of celebrating Billy Graham Day a thousand years from now by wearing powder-blue suits, drinking bourbon, and hitting the sales at local shopping malls.

The way Patrick's legacy is remembered today—wearing green, drinking beer, and hanging cardboard shamrocks in windows—produces in me a feeling of sadness. I'm not sure how to change the way our culture celebrates this holiday, but I'm determined to change how I, and those I serve, celebrate it. In our church, we ask our staff to take a break from any office work and spend the day outside the office serving and building relationships with those who don't yet know Christ.

The fact that people mark the worldwide holiday bearing Patrick's name with celebrations that honor green alcohol, rainbows, and leprechauns rather than the man and his legacy of faith and love proves how uninterested Patrick was in marketing.

SAINTHOOD—NOT THE SAME AS PERFECTION

Occasionally when we review history, we discover a man of faith who transformed culture rather than reading about civilizations reformed through bloodshed. In Patrick we witness a man determined to listen to the voice of God, willing to be misunderstood, and courageous enough to give others his heart and soul.

Author Thomas Cahill aptly describes key figures of influence in the Western world as

> the story of ... the great gift-givers, arriving in the moment of crisis, [providing] for transition, for transformation, and even for transfiguration, leaving us a world more varied and complex, more awesome and delightful, more beautiful and strong than the one they had found.[13]

Patrick certainly fits this description.

But while the title of saint is honoring and celebrative, it doesn't imply perfection. The term *saint* can be complicated and sometimes misunderstood. In the Catholic tradition, before a person can officially be declared a saint, the church puts him or her through an evaluation process, and specific criteria must be met. Specific saints are then identified as those whose lives are worth remembering and imitating.

In a general sense, however, everyone who surrenders their will to God and puts their faith in Jesus is brought from death to life and becomes a saint. The apostle Paul even used the word when describing different roles in the church:

> [God] gave some to be apostles, some prophets,
> some evangelists, and some pastors and teachers, for
> the equipping of the saints for the work of ministry,
> for the edifying of the body of Christ.[14]

Sainthood, in its essence, describes a person who has been set apart for the purposes of godliness. So if you consider yourself a follower of Jesus, you fit the bill.

But I assume you don't do it perfectly.

Patrick was just like you and me. We are all sinners. Failures. We all miss moral targets.

And we are all recipients of grace.

Patrick refused to let the shame of sin hold him back from serving the people God called him to. He trusted the grace of God and pressed on. His view of strength originated not in his manhood but in a Trinitarian being, all-powerful and sovereign.

When we put our trust in the Divine, we can break free from the bondage of our regrets and lean into the love we long to give away.

Some of you have loved and lost. What once had life has burned to the ground. You think about love, and all you see are the charred remains.

In the soil of your grief, love has its greatest opportunity to live again.

Why? Because the protection of the forest is gone. You are raw and exposed. That which you had built up to protect yourself is gone. You are vulnerable.

And love thrives most in vulnerability.

Perhaps your greatest act of vulnerability would be to allow yourself to be loved. To accept that you are indeed worth loving.

Your story is perhaps the hope someone is waiting for.

Consider this prayer of Saint Patrick and let these words speak to your heart:

I arise today
Through the strength of heaven;
Light of the sun,
Splendor of fire,
Speed of lightning,
Swiftness of the wind,
Depth of the sea,
Stability of the earth,
Firmness of the rock.

I arise today
Through God's strength to pilot me;
God's might to uphold me,
God's wisdom to guide me,
God's eye to look before me,
God's ear to hear me,
God's word to speak for me,
God's hand to guard me,
God's way to lie before me,
God's shield to protect me,
God's hosts to save me
From snares of the devil,
From temptations of vices,
From everyone who desires me ill,
Afar and anear,
Alone or in a multitude....

Christ with me, Christ before me, Christ behind me,
Christ in me, Christ beneath me, Christ above me,
Christ on my right, Christ on my left,
Christ when I lie down, Christ when I sit down,
Christ in the heart of every man who thinks of me,
Christ in the mouth of every man who speaks of me,
Christ in the eye that sees me,
Christ in the ear that hears me.

I arise today
Through a mighty strength, the invocation of the Trinity,
Through a belief in the Threeness,
Through a confession of the Oneness
Of the Creator of creation.[15]

As Ashton and I boarded the plane to England to unite with the rest of the team, I reflected on this great saint and how he made an impact on an entire civilization. As I considered the parallels between his life and my own, a question began to take shape in my mind.

Does every great legacy require sacrifice and suffering?

This haunting question would find a reinforced answer in the days ahead.

Chapter 2

EMBRACE YOUR
LIMITATIONS

William Cowper, AD 1731–1800, and
John Newton, AD 1725–1807, Olney, England

His name, his love, his gracious voice have fixed my roving heart.

"My Roving Heart," All Sons & Daughters

After connecting with our team the previous evening, our now-full contingent embarked on our adventure, heading first to Olney, England. As we climbed off the bus, the town's quaint English charm immediately captured us. Centuries-old stone townhomes and antique shops surrounded us as we organized our day in the shade of a majestic oak tree in the village square. Tourists and locals alike mingled nearby with gleeful chatter.

Finally, Leslie and David's manager, Chris, located the entrance to our first stop: the poet William Cowper's former residence turned museum. With the film gear in tow, our team was ready.

The staff members at the Cowper house were lovely. Generous with questions, they asked what brought us across the ocean to their town. Leslie explained how she stumbled upon Cowper's story while researching English poets. Upon learning of the hundreds of hymns he composed and his struggle with debilitating depression, she was immediately drawn in. Within a few moments of our arrival, Paul, the museum curator, arrived and began unraveling a wondrous tale not just of William Cowper but also of another man. It quickly became evident that the story of one man wouldn't be understood without telling the story of the other. And God would use both to inspire the masses.

THE COWRITERS

William Cowper (pronounced "cooper") was a preacher's kid who became one of England's greatest eighteenth-century writers.

Cowper hailed from a prominent family. His father was the rector of Saint Peter's Church in a town north of London, and his family abounded with lawyers. Cowper was about six years old when his mother died. He spent his childhood in boarding school, where older boys abused and molested him. This traumatic experience seemed to hide in the background of his days.

As the years passed by, the pressure to follow in the footsteps of those around him and study law became burdensome for Cowper. He went through the motions but was uninterested in law, nursing a keener desire to study literature. Having struggled with severe depression for years, probably from his childhood trauma, Cowper had a nervous breakdown in his midtwenties. He was admitted to an insane asylum, where he spent the next two years. Cowper emerged from the mental hospital emotionally frail and continued battling bouts of depression throughout his lifetime.

After Cowper's stay in the hospital, a local, retired clergyman named Morley Unwin and his wife, Mary, took him in. When Morley fell from a horse and died, Cowper moved with Mary to the town of Olney. There he became close friends with the local pastor, a man named John Newton, who had helped Mary Unwin and Cowper relocate to a house down the lane from his own.

Cowper developed an unusually close relationship with the older Mrs. Unwin, making some question the nature of their relationship. Living with her in Olney, Cowper dedicated his life to gardening and caring for animals, keeping several rabbits as pets. In light of his emotionally difficult life, it seems that writing was a valuable salve that provided a complementary mélange of expression and hope.

Cowper struggled with shame and insecurity for many years. The concept of grace seemed too gratuitous to receive. But one day, while he sat in his garden, the love of God finally broke through. He wrote, "Immediately I received strength to believe, and the full beams of the Sun of Righteousness shone upon me. I saw the sufficiency of the atonement [Christ] had made, my pardon sealed in his blood, and all the fulness and completeness of his justification. In a moment I believed, and received the gospel."[1]

Newton took great joy in fanning the flame of faith in Cowper's life. He knew what it was like to live apart from the light of Christ.

Newton grew up in a less privileged environment than Cowper. The son of a seafarer, he spent his childhood along the banks of the Thames River in the East End of London. When Newton was six or seven years old, his mother died. Here we find the one thing both men had in common: the absence of a maternal presence during their formative years.

When Newton was eleven, his father took him out to sea on a number of voyages. A rebellious chap, Newton was press-ganged into the Royal Navy at nineteen to apply some discipline and submission to his life. It didn't work. The navy dumped him on a merchant vessel. Eventually Newton found himself in Sierra Leone, where he tried to find employment in the slave trade. Almost penniless, he took a job as a servant to a slave trader. Abused and mistreated along with the slaves, Newton had a miserable experience. Upon hearing about his son's struggles, Newton's father called on some fellow sailors to retrieve him and return him to England.

These men sailed to the coast of Africa on a vessel named the *Greyhound*. After finding the young man, they passed along his father's wishes. Newton resisted. Things had started to turn around for him, and he was now running his own enterprise in human trafficking. He refused to go home, saying that the slave trade was lucrative, and he liked what he was doing.

Determined not to return empty handed, the captain of the *Greyhound* baited Newton with a lie, saying an inheritance awaited him back home. Newton took the bait. Not wanting to miss an opportunity for easy money, he boarded the ship and headed back to England. On that voyage, a massive storm erupted that threatened to destroy the ship and everyone on board. There on the Atlantic Ocean, battling massive waves that tossed the vessel like an unwanted rag doll, this dissolute character found himself powerless to control his circumstances. Newton's narcissism crystallized in that moment, and this great crisis brought him to faith. He called out to God for deliverance and pledged to dedicate his life to the ways of the Divine. Like many who choose to follow God, Newton needed time for his understanding of what this meant to materialize.

Sometimes our moment of conversion is hard to pin down. I had a significant encounter with God at the age of five, guided by the words of my father. I had another as a young middle-school student sitting on the front row of a church listening to the hymn "Turn Your Eyes upon Jesus." Then another as a freshman in high school, sitting with other students listening to stories of revival. I've had many intimate moments with God since then. Which of these was my conversion experience? Honestly, I can't say for certain. What I can say is that I know when my life is dedicated to the will of the Father and when I'm not interested in following His plan. I can point out moments when I've succumbed to the flesh and moments when I've been alive to the Spirit. I could describe for you times in my life that have been hellish and other times that have been heavenly.

James, the brother of Jesus, wrote this: "As the body without the spirit is dead, so faith without works is dead also."[2] We can have a deeply spiritual moment with God, and it can be just that ... a moment. Or God can give us an ongoing life transformation that leaves in its wake spiritual produce. It seems it took Newton some time to understand the difference.

After arriving in England and discovering that the inheritance spiel was a lie, Newton found a job serving as first mate on a slave-trading ship and was eventually promoted to captain. After a number of voyages, he suffered a serious epileptic seizure and was advised to quit sailing. Newton did, and after dabbling in a handful of business ventures, he felt drawn to study theology and enter vocational ministry.

As Newton grew closer to God, he began to see clearly the error of his ways, in particular his participation in the dehumanizing business of human trafficking. Feeling great contrition, he became an important voice in the abolition of slavery in England.

Years later, as a pastor in the small town of Olney, Newton forged a friendship with William Cowper, taking him under his wing. Newton frequently made his way from his vicarage down the lane and through the back gate to Cowper's garden, where he'd encourage Cowper in his Christian faith. An unusual pair, they shared similar backgrounds of redemption and ongoing trust in God that produced great literary insight. Newton and Cowper compiled a collection of songs they had written that were eventually published as the *Olney Hymns*.

Together, a narcissistic captain of a slave ship turned pastor and a depressed poet turned hymn writer inspired and encouraged each other to push through reluctance and regret and give something meaningful to the world.

And the world is better for it.

THE GARDEN

With the story still wafting around us, we entered William Cowper's garden. All the charm of the English tales I had read as a child came to life in a sensory kaleidoscope. Two separate wooden gates guarded the botanical sanctuary, which exploded in color and fragrance from the many plants, herbs, and flowers surrounding us. Our tour guide, Paul, continued his narration, explaining that in maintaining the authenticity of Cowper's residence, the staff had planted the same flowers and greenery the poet had so carefully tended to some 220 years ago.

Still enraptured by the fragrance of perennials and the chirping of birds, we came upon a small stone hut the size of a child's playhouse.

It was Cowper's writing shack, a place he dubbed his "sulking house" and "verse manufactory." In that tiny space, Cowper stammered out his depression in words and phrases, moving his pen in hopes of quieting the debilitating voices in his head.

*Existence is a strange bargain. Life owes
us little; we owe it everything.
The only true happiness comes from
squandering ourselves for a purpose.*

William Cowper

Stepping away from the little enclave, I thought about Newton, envisioning him knocking on the garden gate and letting himself inside Cowper's sanctum. I pictured him offering a silent gaze as Cowper drifted off in contemplation or put pen to paper in creative fury.

Newton, who genuinely cared for his parishioners and had a passion for upholding the dignity of God's creation, seemed undeterred in his determination to keep Cowper writing. Those who spend time around writers lost in the ferocity of sparring words are usually careful to wait for an invitation to speak. When one is locked in creative thought, the last thing a writer wants to do is leave that space abruptly. I imagine there were times Cowper ignored his pastor and kept on writing, and then other times when the poet would look up with a smile, put down his pen, and join the persistent preacher for a stroll through the garden.

I wonder what they talked about. What did they dream of? How often did one of them want to give up what he was doing for a greener pasture? Was this the place where Newton convinced Cowper to compile their hymns? Could either of them have ever imagined that in the centuries to come millions of people, with misty eyes, would sing one of Newton's songs over and over, belting out the profound confession, "I once was lost, but now am found, was blind, but now I see"?

Walking out of the garden, down the lane, and toward Newton's church, I asked our host if he knew where the famed pastor had penned the words to the world's most famous hymn.

"Certainly," he told us.

I was taken slightly aback. Prior to this time, I had never given thought to where "Amazing Grace" might have been written. My own sacred experiences with that hymn made it special to be near its place of origin.

As we turned a corner, Paul pointed to a house with two gables. "There," he said, referencing the upstairs window on the right side of the house. "That was Newton's office and where he wrote the words to 'Amazing Grace.' It was actually written for a New Year's Day sermon given in his church on January 1, 1773."

Incredulous, I turned to David and remarked that in our desire to learn about Cowper, I never imagined the story would trail back to the birthplace of this great hymn. He shook his head and said with a grin, "It's crazy, man."

Newton was an innovator ahead of his time. It wasn't until 1820 that parishioners were allowed to sing hymns in a church edifice. Until that time, chanting was the only form of musical expression that church leaders deemed appropriate. Newton, however, felt otherwise. While working in Sierra Leone, he witnessed how music lifted the spirits of the slaves and was convinced it could do the same for his flock. So to offer Christians the opportunity to worship God through song,

Newton held services in an unoccupied mansion next to the church building.

What creativity! Rather than rebel against the church, Newton found an alternative solution. "Every creative endeavor becomes a realization of both how limited and how unlimited we are.... One of the great misconceptions about [art] is that it only exists where there are no rules, no boundaries, and no limitations.... [Some people are] convinced that creativity blooms only when we are free of boundaries."[3]

OUR CONTEXT IS OUR CANVAS

I've spoken with many mothers who find themselves creatively unsatisfied. While rearing children is meaningful and life giving, it has limited their ability to pursue specific goals, dreams, and opportunities for artistic expression.

I've spoken with singles who are frustrated with the absence of a significant other in their lives. They long to share their lives with someone else and feel discouraged without a companion by their side.

I've spoken with professionals who have dreams but are disappointed with their lack of margin to fan the flame of dormant creativity. They want to get back to their guitars, photography, song writing, design, and painting but are too exhausted from their workdays to find a way to reengage.

We each face obstacles that are more than perceived. They're real.

And they are meant to be there.

Our context is the canvas for our creativity.

Erwin McManus observes in *The Artisan Soul*, "There is always context for art. Every medium carries within itself inherent limitations, and every artist also comes with limitations.... Creativity not only happens within boundaries and limitations, but in fact it is dependent on those limitations. The true artist sees boundaries not as the materials denied to us but as the material that allows us to harness and focus our full creative potential."[4]

Contexts have restraints, just as all mediums have constraints. Whether we work with clay, words, stone, paint, or music, we're limited in what we can create.

And thus we come to an important life principle: *embrace your limitations.*

I first heard this phrase from my friend Nick, a music manager. My sons are musicians. For the past two years, they've been plugging away in the general market as indie artists. Most of their energy and marketing has ridden the wave of social media. Nick, who has been a mentor to my sons, reminds them often to embrace their limitations.

Nick has suggested that rather than spend their energy on attempting to book large venues, they stay ambitious but play the small ones instead. He advises them to make personal connections with fans as long as they can. Act spontaneously. He posits that the greater their success, the less these luxuries will be available to them. Nick reminds my sons to savor each stage of their journey, to enjoy the nuances. Life is full of trade-offs, he says, and one day the freedom that comes with being a young band will become a distant memory.

We're all limited in varying degrees. But that doesn't have to squash our innate drive to uniquely create, to make a difference, to effect change.

If somewhere in your story someone told you that you weren't creative, please know that is simply not true. Researcher Brené Brown writes, "'I'm not very creative' doesn't work. There's no such thing as creative people and non-creative people. There are only people who use their creativity and people who don't. Unused creativity doesn't just disappear. It lives within us until it's expressed, neglected to death, or suffocated by resentment and fear."[5]

The first creative act in Scripture was a spoken word that created contrast.

"Let there be light" (Gen. 1:3). A universe followed. Then a planet, and then creatures on that planet, as well as natural limitations, rules, laws, and restrictions. God created an atmosphere that bears within it a delicate balance of elements and chemicals.

Gravity is both a gift and a limitation.

God created man and woman, creatures made in His likeness and yet limited in capacity. Men and women are equal in value but vary in physiology and proclivity. They share a common humanity and yet carry distinction.

It isn't accidental that God formed one from the dust and one from a rib.

Embrace the limitations of being a woman. Or being a man.

Embrace the limitations of being a mother. Or not being one.

If you're in a season of productivity, produce and be grateful for the opportunity to see the fruit of your labor.

If you're in a season of slowing, choose to enjoy the subtleties of beauty. Sketch a leaf, smell the honeysuckle, carve a pumpkin or ten of them. Lie in the grass and feel the earth. Sit in a snowdrift and absorb the silence.

Recognize that each limitation points toward something of value in your life. And remember, a limitation today may not be one tomorrow.

> *The man who can articulate the movements of his inner life ... need no longer be a victim of himself, but is able slowly and consistently to remove the obstacles that prevent the spirit from entering.*[6]
> Henri Nouwen

John Newton could have crumbled in shame over his involvement in the slave trade. Instead, he dedicated his life to abolishing it. He influenced a young British politician named William Wilberforce, who became the voice of the abolition movement in Parliament. Newton's encouragement and Wilberforce's courage were instrumental in putting an end to slavery in England. In addition to being involved in this movement and writing what is arguably the world's most famous hymn, Newton pastored churches and encouraged others to express their creativity with focused purpose.

William Cowper could have wallowed in his victimization, and it seems he did at times. Yet over and over, like a prizefighter, he had the courage to get back on his feet and stay in the fight.

Today Cowper is considered one of England's most respected poets. Other writers, such as Robert Burns, Jane Austen, William Wordsworth, William Blake, George Eliot, Alfred Lord Tennyson, and Virginia Woolf, loved and admired him. But even with this great success, he was never quite able to overcome the ache of life.

Newton and Cowper both lived with limitations. Newton lived continually with the regret and shame of having been a slave trader. Cowper battled depression and was at times suicidal throughout his life.

Together, however, these men faced their fears, pushed through their sadness, and contributed to the love story of God.

Though we might smile and soak up the hope revealed so majestically through the words of the poets and saints who have gone before us, we often forget about the pain and failure in their personal lives.

God used Cowper's pain to bring Himself glory. Newton's redemption gave hope to the people he once abused.

As the members of our team gathered their belongings and returned to the bus, I hung back in the garden a few more minutes, watching my lovely daughter walk past the tulips. Then, lifting my eyes, I asked the Lord,

Have I done enough?

Where am I stuck?

What don't I see?

What am I afraid of?

What tape keeps playing in my head about my inadequacy?

What subtleties of creation am I screaming past and failing to notice?

Pulling my gaze from the clouds and back to the lush vegetation around me, I said aloud, "I think I need a garden."

I might have heard the Spirit whisper back, *You were made for one.*

Chapter 3

TO BE SEEN
AND KNOWN

C. S. Lewis, AD 1898–1963, Oxford, England

Halleluiahs rising like the daylight, heaven meets earth.
"Heaven Meets Earth," All Sons & Daughters

When I was around the age of ten, my parents bought me a boxed set of C. S. Lewis's The Chronicles of Narnia. As promised on the packaging, after I read one book in the series, I wanted to read them all. Lewis gently carried my imagination into the wild and mystical land of Narnia. In this world of centaurs and elves and talking beasts, a child can be lost and found, scared and comforted. And while *redemption* is a word most kids don't use, when entering the world of Narnia, they quickly feel its power.

I identified with the mythical characters Lewis so affectionately depicted in the series. Aslan, the dangerous yet kindhearted lion who represented God, felt congruent with my own understanding of a compassionate deity, the one to whom I directed my bedtime prayers. I suppose many things shape our views of the Divine, and looking back I owe a great deal to Lewis's portrayal of God's strength, power, and gentleness in my early adolescent, ever-evolving view of Him.

THE RELUCTANT CONVERT

Born on November 29, 1898, in Belfast, Ireland, Clive Staples Lewis wasn't interested in being a Christ follower for a significant part of his life. Nor did he set out to be a Christian apologist or philosopher, as he is known today.

As a young man, Lewis suffered his mother's death and the alienation of his father, experiences that diminished any belief he may have had in God. A tutor by the name of W. T. Kirkpatrick introduced Lewis, who was deeply philosophical and an avid reader, to classical literature and taught him to criticize, analyze, and think and write logically. This training reinforced Lewis's decision to be an atheist. With Kirkpatrick's strong tutelage, Lewis was accepted to Oxford University, where he became a student in 1917.

A year later, like most young English men of his time, Lewis served as a soldier in the First World War. After being wounded on Mount Berenchon during the Battle of Arras and becoming disgusted with the boredom and carnage of war, Lewis returned to Oxford to pursue intellectual interests with fervor. He published his first book, *Spirits in Bondage*, in 1919 under the pseudonym Clive Hamilton.

While teaching and writing at Oxford, Lewis conceded that his athe-istic worldview was deteriorating. Important questions were met only with inferior answers. He was also beginning to recognize that men of great intellect embraced spirituality. Unable to ignore the Christian wisdom of the ages, he sensed the Spirit of God speaking through poets and saints, such as George MacDonald, G. K. Chesterton, John Milton, Julian of Norwich, Saint Augustine, and others, which dis-rupted his atheistic pretense and dispelled his disbelief. Lewis began to look upward and inward.

The things I assert most vigorously are those
that I resisted long and accepted late.[1]

C. S. Lewis

He resisted "the hound of heaven" until one night he could resist no longer. He wrote, "You must picture me alone in that room in Magdalen [College], night after night, feeling, whenever my mind lifted even for a second from my work, the steady, unrelenting approach of Him whom I so earnestly desired not to meet. That which I greatly feared had at last come upon me. In the Trinity Term of 1929 I gave in, and admitted that God was God, and knelt and prayed: perhaps, that night, the most dejected and reluctant convert in all England."[2]

As Lewis plunged into a submissive relationship with the Creator, his bright intellect and sociological intuition pushed him to continue to question and interrogate the Christian faith. Believing there was a God was just the first step. He now had to wrestle down the deity of Jesus. At age thirty-three, after a long talk one night with friends, including

J. R. R. Tolkien and Hugo Dyson, Lewis accepted that Jesus was indeed the Son of God. For the next sixteen years, along with studying literature, language, and logic, Lewis discussed faith with his friends and came to understand the impact of the biblical narrative on every facet of life.

WHO IS THIS GOD?

In 1956, Lewis married an American writer named Joy Davidman. The marriage greatly disrupted the old bachelor's way of life. Joy's two sons provided Lewis with an instant family, just what he needed. In embracing his new life, Lewis shed his self-centered routine. When Joy, with whom he was deeply in love, died of cancer only four years after they married, he was heartbroken.

In his book *A Grief Observed*, Lewis wrote, "God has not been trying an experiment on my faith or love in order to find out their quality. He knew it already. It was I who didn't. In this trial He makes us occupy the dock, the witness box, and the bench all at once. He always knew that my temple was a house of cards. His only way of making me realize the fact was to knock it down."[3]

Throughout Lewis's life and, in particular, because of Joy's death, Lewis searched for truth. Willing to play his part in the divine production, he also needed to know and be able to trust the character of God.

What kind of God knocks down our house of cards?

Is He a sadist?

Does He want us to pay for the pain humanity has put Him through?

No, these aren't the motives of a rambunctious, playful, loving, eternal Father. God allows and orchestrates struggle to shape us into spiritual athletes, warriors, and professional artisans.

Consider this:

Which player do you want on your team? The one who has never been tested, or the one who has experience?

Which soldier do you want to protect you or fight alongside you in battle? The green private from boot camp, or the veteran who has bled on the battlefield?

Why are you willing to spend more and listen longer to a professional artist as opposed to an amateur?

Pain unlocks perspective.

We see the world differently when we've suffered. When we share what we've learned from our pain, we give others the gift of hope.

INSPIRED WARRIORS

When my now-nineteen-year-old twin sons, Jordan and Tyler, were around nine, I introduced them to the magical world of Narnia. They, too, were enthralled by the sweeping adventure of the great man's writings.

A short time later, J. R. R. Tolkien, a poet, writer, and scholar who happened to be one of Lewis's good friends, activated our imaginations. When the stories of his Lord of the Rings trilogy were adapted to film and the first trailer hit the screens, we as a family greatly anticipated the visual jubilee of the mythic motion pictures.

We weren't disappointed.

The movies made us instant Tolkien fans, and my boys begged for more of his books and trilogy novelties. Before long Tyler donned the elvish attire of Legolas and Jordan started dressing up as Aragorn. Our home videos pay tribute to our sons living out their fantasies as young warriors of Middle Earth.

As the twins moved through adolescence, their mother and I couldn't help but notice that in many ways their personalities were a lot like their heroes. Though reluctant, Jordan carried a leadership mantle that couldn't be ignored. Tyler was a cautious, analytical observer, much more interested in the precision of an arrow than the indiscriminate slashing of a broadsword.

When the boys graduated high school, my wife and I presented them with replicas of the weapons their childhood heroes wielded. In the spirit of our dramatic gifts, I gave them this somewhat tongue-in-cheek charge:

"Jordan, you have so many of the characteristics of a firstborn. Anduril, the sword of Aragorn, which to this day is still your email address, is a broadsword that symbolizes the way you approach life. You swing hard, and you swing fast. And then you evaluate the success or damage. You aren't afraid to be at the very front of the line. Courage abounds in you, and that is the sign of a leader.

"Tyler, you have the mind of a strategist. You are selective. Like Legolas, you take aim with the intention of making every shot true. His bow and arrow and his white knives were designed and used for precision. Your physical bravery and your analytical mind allow you to look ahead and see what others don't see. You also have all the markings of a leader."

I concluded with one of Tolkien's famous lines: "All [you] have to decide is what to do with the time that is given [you]."[4]

THE EAGLE AND CHILD

Lewis and Tolkien seemed to have that same kind of warrior bond. Though they weren't twin brothers, the affection they had for each other was honorable and enduring. Lewis had a deep respect for friendship. In his book *The Four Loves*, he described it as "that luminous, tranquil, rational world of relationships freely chosen."[5]

The bond that Lewis and Tolkien enjoyed spread to other literary enthusiasts. This handful of writers met over pints of ale and indulged in conversations as wide ranging as "red-brick universities ... torture, Tertullian, bores, the contractual theory of mediaeval kingship, and odd place-names."[6] Before long this group would be known as the Inklings: "In general, the all-male group shared a longing for that half-imaginary time before man's alienation from God, nature and self, the time before the chaos and materialism of the post-industrial era had displaced the elegantly organized cosmos of the Middle Ages."[7] The Inklings met regularly for nearly two decades. When they weren't gathering in someone's study, they often convened in a pub called the Eagle and Child.

In light of my admiration for both Lewis and Tolkien, you may understand my fervor when I learned this legendary venue was on our itinerary. Walking up to this traditional English pub in the heart of Oxford, I wasn't the only one filled with excitement. Leslie (songwriter, musician, and catalyst for this project) and Sarah (our team's artist and researcher) were just as fascinated.

The Eagle and Child had the feel and look of a place that had served its share of beverages. The wooden tables had been polished to a smooth sheen from elbows and forearms resting on the surface between countless bites and gestures. The ceilings were low, giving the place a cave-like quality. We paused at the historic Rabbit Room, where many conversations between Lewis and Tolkien ostensibly took place; then we meandered to the back of the pub for fish and chips.

VULNERABILITY BREEDS VULNERABILITY

Our director, Zach, and our cameraman, Matt, set up their gear at the Eagle and Child, positioning one camera in the center of the room and prepping the other for an OTS (over-the-shoulder) shot. After adjusting the mic levels to record in a rowdy pub, they began shooting while Leslie, David, Sarah, and I reflected on our appreciation for Lewis and how he had affected our lives.

Sarah discussed Lewis's last work of fiction, *Till We Have Faces*, a book based on the mythical love story of Cupid and Psyche. In several letters with friends, Lewis wrote that, in his opinion, this book was his best literary creation. So he understandably felt a bit of confusion and sadness when it met with an uncelebrated reception upon publication. Critics and the public alike considered the novel a failure. Yet although it doesn't have the readership of, say, The Chronicles of Narnia, *Till We Have Faces* has, in fact, stood the test of time.

After spending the past twenty-five years in the soil of people's lives and dealing with my own human frailty, I suspect that many readers are uncomfortable with the powerful truth that confronts them in this great tale. Lewis chronicled the story of Orual, a woman who lives with a veil shrouding her face because she feels great shame from her physical imperfections and other shortcomings. This veil is her fabricated, self-made persona. It not only masks her true identity; it also acts as a shield that protects her from being truly known by others.

Orual recalls her teacher saying to her, "Child, to say the very thing you really mean, the whole of it, nothing more or less or other than what you really mean; that's the whole art and joy of words." Orual reflects on this truth: "Till that word can be dug out of us, why should they [the gods] hear the babble that we think we mean? How can they meet us face to face till we have faces?"[8]

In a climactic moment, Orual stands before the gods, squirming behind her opaque covering. Her mask doesn't fool them. In that moment she is confronted with a choice: remain behind the veil and never be truly known, or remove it and expose her face, her true self, before them.

Vulnerability doesn't come easy. But when it comes, it brings life.

Sitting around the table in this legendary pub, each of us chimed in about how we desire to be our authentic selves, and how hard that can be.

I talked about how I have a tendency to qualify what I say to soften the blow of my words for the one with whom I might disagree.

Leslie shared about when she first started leading worship in our church. Right after the service was over, she would pack up her guitar as quickly as possible and sneak out the back door lest anyone stop her and ask questions she wasn't sure she could answer.

Sarah talked about how she's tempted to stay silent during conflict. She can't say anything wrong if she doesn't say anything at all.

David admitted that being part of a docu-study like this project was intimidating. Because he's passionate about music and production, not books, he feared he would have nothing to contribute.

As friends who shared a common purpose, we were experiencing ourselves as brothers and sisters in the family of God. Not only was it safe to be vulnerable about our shortcomings; it was also freeing. In that moment we were removing our veils. Our masks were off. And as we revealed our fears, they lost their power.

I spoke directly.

Leslie stayed put.

Sarah spoke up.

David contributed.

Brené Brown notes that "we cultivate love when we allow our most vulnerable and powerful selves to be deeply seen and known, and when we honor the spiritual connection that grows from that offering with trust, respect, kindness, and affection. Love is not something we give or get; it is something that we nurture and grow, a connection that can only be cultivated between two people when it exists within each one of them."[9]

We have such high expectations for people, don't we? The way they park their vehicles, their level of politeness at a drive-through window, the size of their smiles when they greet us at the front door of a church. And the ones closest to us? How often do we push them away in our determination to get them to conform to our image? Constant evaluation and incessant reminders of shortcomings produce constraint, limitation, and shame, not freedom and reciprocity.

Love doesn't force.

Love keeps no record of wrongs.

Love hopes.

Love invites.

There is no such thing as instant community. A relationship is an experience built on moments of relating. The greater the accumulation and flavor of these moments, the deeper the relationship. The more we let go of our perfectionism, the more honest and genuine those moments will be.

TRUE IDENTITY

I'm struck by something Orual said in Lewis's myth. She asked how intimacy with the gods is possible if we don't know who we are. I wonder if this is one of life's great quests, discovering and leaning into who we are meant to be. I'm not sure on this side of heaven if I'll ever understand my true identity, but I do know one thing: I'm closest to my real self when I enter the cross fire of the Trinity. When I'm caught up in their love exchange, I'm carried to another Kingdom. It is then I am most at peace and most myself.

When was the last time you caught a glimpse of your true self?

When was the last time you felt comfortable in your own skin?

When did you last feel truly connected? You knew, at least momentarily, the reason you were on this planet.

Years ago I coached a soccer team at a small school in New York. Many of the kids who tried out had never played the sport. As they ran the field and worked on their drills, I'd occasionally notice certain players who had obvious talent. With arms crossed, I'd stand on the sidelines, point out one particular young man, and remark to the assistant coach next to me, "Now, that kid; he's got potential." Coaches all over the world make that statement about athletes. What does it mean?

It means we see something in someone else.

He has a unique drive.

She has great stamina.

He's easily coached.

She's naturally athletic.

He has spirit.

She can hustle.

And often it means we see something in people that they can't see themselves.

Did you know that only God knows your full potential?

We are God's handiwork, created in Christ Jesus to do good
works, which God prepared in advance for us to do.[10]
Paul the apostle

"You can be anything you want to be" is a nice line from a motivational speaker, but it's not accurate. And this is a humbling thing to accept.

If you're a bush, you can't be a tree. If you're a meadow, you can't be a desert. "You will always be you—a growing, healthy you or a languishing you—but God did not create you to be anybody else."[11]

You know what's interesting? We often resist the thing we're really good at. You might argue, "But people say you should follow your passions!"

Sure, follow your passions. Until you get redirected.

I wanted to be a stuntman for *The A-Team*. But that didn't work out.

MODERN-DAY POETS

With some free time after dinner, Sarah, Ashton, and I went for a walk through Oxford. Flanking us were huge Gothic steeples, and formidable, caramel-colored buildings stood like sentinels one after the other. It seemed as if we were walking through the set of *Harry*

Potter, which we learned had been filmed nearby. Ashton was determined to find a sweatshirt, while Sarah and I were intent on finding Blackwell's, a well-known Oxford bookstore. Each of us managed to find something to take back home with us, and we returned to the bus quite content.

When the rest of the gang arrived, talking about how much fun they had walking the streets of Oxford, Sarah made an imaginative suggestion about sharing a favorite song.

She said, "Were you to continue walking outside and had to play one song that described how you felt, what would it be?"

We all jumped on our iPhones and started scrolling through our lists of contemporary musical poets. Then, one by one we connected to the Bluetooth in the bus lounge and played our songs. We oohed and aahed and laughed. Zach interrupted us once to blurt out, "This just might be my favorite thing to do ... ever!"

Following is the eclectic playlist from our diverse ensemble of travelers:

Thomas—"Tunnels" by Angels & Airwaves

Leslie —"Kids" by Mikky Ekko

David—"Guiding Light" by Foy Vance

Natalie—"Style" by Taylor Swift

Matt—"Between Me and You" by Brandon Flowers

Chris—"Thankful" by Jonny Lang

Zach—"Live While We're Young" by Johnnyswim

Ashton—"100 Years" by Five for Fighting

Cara—"Holy Ghost" by John Mark McMillan

Sarah—"Rattlesnake" by St. Vincent

Me—"Walt Grace's Submarine Test" by John Mayer

I climbed into my bunk that night and lay there smiling, cherishing the day. My mind drifted off to an imaginary forested plateau and a magnificent untamed lion ...

> He stood for a second, his eyes very bright, his limbs quivering, lashing himself with his tail. Then he made a leap high over their heads and landed on the other side of the Table. Laughing, though she didn't know why, Lucy scrambled over it to reach him. Aslan leaped again. A mad chase began. Round and round the hill-top he led them, now hopelessly out of their reach, now letting them almost catch his tail, now diving between them, now tossing them in the air with his huge and beautifully velveted

paws and catching them again, and now stopping unexpectedly so that all three of them rolled over together in a happy laughing heap of fur and arms and legs. It was such a romp as no one has ever had except in Narnia.[12]

Chapter 4

EVERY MOMENT
IS A GIFT

George MacDonald, AD 1824–1905, London, England

Though dim I am still a reflection of mercy and of truth.

"I Wait," All Sons & Daughters

The next morning we were still reflecting on the fun we had and how songs can so easily capture and express our feelings in the moment. Sarah elaborated on how one of her artistic influences, Patty Griffin, changed the way she experienced music. She said that, sadly, many artists like Patty have musical genius that mainstream music virtually ignores. Some of the others agreed. As they discussed artists from Donny Hathaway to Paper Route, I noticed their voice inflections change to an almost reverent tone. Regardless of their varying tastes in pop music, they all seemed to agree that there are rare musicians who transcend taste and preference. And despite being mostly unknown to pop-culture media, they are deeply respected by those who create it.

It seems some are called to exist as sunlight under the horizon. They have talent. Loads of it. But for whatever reason, their art form inspires other artists rather than the masses.

Some are meant to create art for art's sake. Their artistic renderings carry an elegance—even a supremacy. Perhaps this is why the common consumer fails to notice. Without an appreciation for the depth, character, and complexity of the music, the pedestrian will glance, shrug, and disregard the art like a homeowner selling a precious heirloom at a garage sale, unaware of its value.

Though the masses have by no means ignored George MacDonald, the Scottish poet and storyteller from Aberdeenshire, Scotland, a fair share of the uninformed have overlooked him.

Great thinkers, philosophers, and writers of the twentieth century have found inspiration in this man's word craft. Many of these have become household names, including C. S. Lewis and J. R. R. Tolkien, as well as Mark Twain, Madeleine L'Engle, and G. K. Chesterton. Chesterton, whom *Time* magazine called "a man of colossal genius,"[1] said that MacDonald's book *The Princess and the Goblin* "made a difference to my whole existence."[2]

A CHANGE IN DIRECTION

Unlike many of the great men we were to study on our trip, George MacDonald had a wonderful relationship with his father and deeply respected him. "From his own father ... he first learned that

Fatherhood must be at the core of the universe. He was thus prepared in an unusual way to teach that religion in which the relation of Father and Son is of all relations the most central."[3]

When MacDonald initially attempted to marry his girlfriend, Louisa, he had a very different paternal experience. The young woman's father thwarted their plans because he didn't believe MacDonald was good enough or would be prosperous enough for his daughter. In spite of her father's resistance, Louisa eventually married MacDonald, and they had eleven children together.

MacDonald's first job out of college was pastoring Trinity Congregational Church in Arundel, England. The majority of his congregation loved him. The church leaders, however, being devoted followers of John Calvin's teachings, were endlessly frustrated with him. For one thing, MacDonald didn't agree with Calvin's doctrine of predestination, the belief that only select humans, "the elect" as Calvin called them, could access the grace of God. MacDonald couldn't conceive of a God who didn't offer salvation to all. This theological difference of opinion became a deep source of contention.

Only a few years passed when the leadership, in an attempt to manipulate MacDonald into leaving the church, reduced his salary significantly. The underhanded scheme didn't work at first, but eventually, at twenty-nine years of age, MacDonald resigned. Broke and without a job, he was unable to support his growing family. His father-in-law's prophecy seemed to come true.

*Division has done more to hide Christ
from the view of all men than all the
infidelity that has ever been spoken.*[4]

George MacDonald

Ostracized from the church and yet still passionate for God, MacDonald needed to find a different outlet for his spiritual energy.

Have you ever been in that place? Misunderstood? Undervalued and unappreciated?

Have you been through an experience in which you did the right thing but paid dearly for it?

Sitting under a massive tree in London's famous Hyde Park, our team discussed what it meant to live life in the shadows, grappling with the feeling of being unknown or unacknowledged.

The spouses in our group—Chris's wife, Brea; David's spouse, Natalie; and Leslie's husband, Thomas—spoke up and acknowledged the difficulty of being married to professionals who are well known for their craft.

Brea talked about how at times she seems lost in the routine of motherhood. She often feels lonely and insignificant. Moving back and forth from bathroom duty to toddler chef, she sees the parenting yield as hard to measure at the end of a day. When it comes to raising children, sometimes only the long view makes life feel meaningful.

EVERY MOMENT IS A GIFT

Natalie shared how the separation that comes with the touring life is difficult but talked passionately about how she loves watching her husband pursue his dreams. While she cares for their daughter and enjoys her teaching career, she also celebrates with David. She sees herself as his support and feels a part of his success.

Thomas discussed what it was like choosing to give up his teaching job to run the lights and pack the gear. He spoke about how hard it was to leave Hawaii, a paradise he loved, and move to Nashville with Leslie as she followed God's calling to write music and lead worship. Thomas shared that he fully supports Leslie, though much of his future is unknown. He's still searching for what career path God might have in store for him.

What we do in the background has an impact and significance most of us will rarely know about. Maybe this is what Jesus meant when He said that in the Kingdom way, the first will be last.[5]

AN INVITATION TO PARTICIPATE

One of the ways George MacDonald was remarkable was his ability to sidestep hatred and find the good in all things. Though his family suffered through seasons of poverty, he found joy in his children's playful imaginations. Though he struggled with his health throughout his life, he channeled his pain and discomfort into his fictional characters. Though he had been compelled to resign from a church, he didn't give up on the church. He chose to find value in deprivation, poor health, and even disagreeable theology: "MacDonald illustrates [in his fictional characters], ... the unshakeable truth that to forgive is to know. He who loves, sees."[6]

After leaving the church, MacDonald was unable to land another job immediately, so he pursued writing. His first work, a book-length poem titled *Within and Without*, was published when he was thirty-one. Three years later, in 1858, he published a mythical tale for adults called *Phantastes*. In it the narrator, Anodos, embarks on a journey in fairyland, where he encounters a shadow demon, tree spirits, invisible hands, and a magical castle. The tale's detailed world of enchantment, full of allegory and moral truths, achieved great success and catapulted MacDonald's career as a fiction writer.

C. S. Lewis randomly picked up *Phantastes* at a train station as a young man and read it. Later he wrote, "It was as if I were carried sleeping across the frontier, or as if I had died in the old country and could never remember how I came alive in the new.... I did not yet know (and I was long in learning) the name of the new quality, the bright shadow, that rested on the travels of Anodos. I do now. It was Holiness.... It was as though the voice which had called to me from the world's end were now speaking at my side."[7]

MacDonald's influence contributed to Lewis's finding Christ and creating mystical literature of his own. I wonder how different the world would be had Lewis not picked up MacDonald's book that day.

This is a prime example of one man's gift shaping another man's legacy. King Solomon once wrote, "What has been will be again, what has been done will be done again; there is nothing new under the sun."[8] We each borrow from the inspiration of another. We only reframe what others have spoken. And so we must be careful not to take ourselves too seriously.

When you're tempted to think you have little worth or nothing of value to offer, remember this: We're meant to write, sing, sculpt, design, craft, parent, clean, and study in *our* own way. No one else's. We aren't duplicators; we're interpreters. The goal is never to live someone else's life. We're meant to give back to the world out of our own stories, whatever they may be.

Whether or not we see it, we've each been invited to participate in the love story of God. We each have something to contribute. We have good works to live out, deeds prepared a long time ago in a Kingdom close at hand.

"Every good endeavor, even the simplest ones, pursued in response to God's calling, can matter forever.... There is a future healed world that he will bring about, and your work is showing it (in part) to others. Your work will be only partially successful, on your *best* days, in bringing that world about."[9]

> *Therefore a thousand stages, each in itself all but*
> *valueless, are of inestimable worth as the necessary and*
> *connected gradations of an infinite progress.*[10]
> George MacDonald

MacDonald believed we are daily living into God's sculpted image for us. Perhaps this is why he chose to stay in motion and keep writing.

There were times his family was on the brink of starvation. He kept writing.

With his diseased lungs, he had difficulty breathing. He kept writing.

He loved being in the moment, but those moments faded. No matter. They were worth writing about.

There is hope in this. We can get distracted with all the reasons why it's too difficult to give ourselves to our work. Financial pressure, pain, rationalization, procrastination—these are all obstacles. I believe the greatest struggle for many of us is simply perfectionism. We can get paralyzed creating anything of value when we fail to realize that we'll only ever be partially successful. Something can always be better. This is not to say we must dismiss excellence or be content with mediocrity, but rather we must accept that perfection is only God's to own. And it's impossible for us to know what God is really up to over the long haul.

What would it be like to give up achieving perfection today and instead live into only what God has in mind for you to be? Today. Not worrying about tomorrow. Letting tomorrow take care of itself. Simply and contentedly allowing yourself to be formed into today's "gradation."

Editing reel-to-reel films in college didn't seem relevant to my calling to be in church ministry. What I didn't know, however, was that during the countless hours I spent editing, my eye was being trained to notice the nuances and beat patterns of story. I couldn't have foreseen that years later when I was studying and teaching the Bible, my eye would pick up those same patterns. Stories came to life for me in ways they didn't for others.

While I was making minimum wage in a film booth, my teaching skills were being honed.

I believe this is true regardless of the station, the job, or the circumstances we're in. We're the beneficiaries of the moment. Would we but rein in our striving and cease our complaining, we would have eyes to see the value that surrounds us.

I'm not saying that dreams are unimportant. I'm saying that the moment you're in has greater significance than you can possibly imagine.

What is in front of you right now?

Some of us, preoccupied with the careers we long for, fail to value the careers we're in. Others, in their longing for another child, or in their grief for a child who has passed on, are looking past the child standing right in front of them. Hug that child. Look into his or her eyes.

"[MacDonald's] peace of mind came not from building on the future but from resting in what he called 'the holy Present.'"[11]

GOD ACTUALLY LIKES US

It's ironic. We've become the beneficiaries of MacDonald's inflexible church leaders. Had the higher-ups not pushed him into leaving, this acclaimed writer might have never written. He certainly wouldn't have had the margin to produce more than fifty published works, vast volumes of thought that have spread like dandelion seeds to the ends of the earth.

It's often in failure and misdirection that we discover we're good at something. Sometimes when we get lost, we find something we otherwise wouldn't have found.

> *I find that the doing of the will of God leaves me*
> *no time to be disputing about His plans.*[12]
>
> George MacDonald

Some of us fail to find the good in the bad because resentment is a shortcut to resolution.

Rather than contributing to the common good or panning for gold in the river of rejection, we get lost in our own little worlds and lose sight of true sovereignty. When someone says, "I have no hope," they're really saying, "I have no more faith." They're blaming God and saying, with their actions at least, that He is incapable of helping them.

What most of us don't understand is that submission is an internal choice, not an external one.

MacDonald could have lived as a victim of the church. Instead, he chose to give back to the church by expressing his convictions through metaphor, poetry, and philosophical acumen. In offering his gift of prose, his attitude wasn't combative but was one of service. There is humility in this way of living. Many of us live our lives trying to figure out what we can do to get God to like us. MacDonald's writing comes across with a sense of inner confidence. He seemed to know that God liked him.

The idea that God likes us is often difficult and humbling to accept. We prefer rules. We prefer religion. We like to think some type of competition is involved. We have to earn something, win something, do something to achieve salvation.

It's hard to believe we could be loved or liked without doing something first to earn it.

Yet according to our Christian Holy Book, "Long before he [God] laid down earth's foundations, he had us in mind, had settled on us as the focus of his love, to be made whole and holy by his love. Long, long ago he decided to adopt us into his family through Jesus Christ. (What pleasure he took in planning this!) He wanted us to enter into the celebration of his lavish gift-giving by the hand of his beloved Son."[13]

THE GOODNESS OF GOD

One day I sat down with my friend Brad and listened as he shared a bit of his story. He told me that God had given him the gift of comedy, and after a long time of resisting, he chose to accept this mantle.

I told him, "Man, I can relate. I often see myself as not worthy enough to receive a gift from God."

Brad made a strange face and in an almost abrasive tone said, "How insulting!" (My friend is a direct sort of guy.) "The God of the universe chooses to give you a gift, and you tell Him He doesn't know what He's doing?"

I squirmed in my chair. "But I'm not sure I'm the right one."

Brad pressed in. "That's not for you to determine. It's not your story. It's God's story. Live out the role He has chosen for you!"

Have you ever told God that you can't submit to His goodness? It's just too good.

I have. There have been times in my life when I felt unworthy to be loved and blessed.

Maybe you've felt this way too. You're fine with suffering but not goodness. We must learn to bear "the weight of glory and the burden of sin simultaneously."[14]

A certain young lady in Scripture understood this. Her story is often remembered around the celebration of Christmas. She never said, "I'm not worthy" because that wasn't the point.

> God sent the angel Gabriel to Nazareth, a town in Galilee, to a virgin pledged to be married to a man named Joseph, a descendant of David. The virgin's name was Mary. The angel went to her and said, "Greetings, you who are highly favored! The Lord is with you."

Mary was greatly troubled at his words and wondered what kind of greeting this might be. But
the angel said to her, "Do not be afraid, Mary;
you have found favor with God. You will conceive
and give birth to a son, and you are to call him
Jesus. He will be great and will be called the Son
of the Most High. The Lord God will give him
the throne of his father David, and he will reign
over Jacob's descendants forever; his kingdom will
never end."

"How will this be," Mary asked the angel, "since I
am a virgin?"

The angel answered, "The Holy Spirit will come
on you, and the power of the Most High will
overshadow you. So the holy one to be born will
be called the Son of God. Even Elizabeth your
relative is going to have a child in her old age, and
she who was said to be unable to conceive is in her
sixth month. For no word from God will ever fail."

"I am the Lord's servant," Mary answered. "May
your word to me be fulfilled."[15]

What a beautiful turn in the story. Mary submitted to the One on
the throne, and the One on the throne submitted His position of
authority to the will of the Father and then left the throne to enter

this teenager's womb. Jesus deferred access to His power and surrendered to His Father, showing us, in effect, how it's done.

Jesus modeled a life of submission.

Perfectly.

AN UNEXPECTED GIFT

Recently a friend of mine introduced me to a married couple, Brian and Sally. They were, among other things, collectors of ancient artifacts. Thinking my wife and I might be interested in his collection, Brian invited us, as well as a handful of others, over one night. Angie and I weren't entirely sure what we were getting ourselves into, but the invitation stoked our curiosity.

We drove to Hendersonville, a town north of Nashville that for years has been known as the home of legendary musician Johnny Cash. (Recently another musician, a young lady named Taylor Swift, also brought fame to the town.) Angie and I, along with the other guests, walked to the front door, and our soon-to-be new friends Brian and Sally welcomed us warmly. Brian's collection of artifacts began with the newly restored house we had just entered. He gave us a brief tour of the charming home, called the Mama Cash House because it was the house Johnny Cash bought his mother. As we entered the living room, Brian pointed out interesting memorabilia from Johnny's life. We knew at some point Brian was going to introduce us to several ancient biblical artifacts, but we quickly learned that Brian has multifarious taste.

While visiting the master bedroom, I turned to my right, stunned at what I saw. "Uh, Brian?" I asked. "Is that Christopher Reeve?"

"Oh yeah, that's his wax replica," Brian replied nonchalantly. "The Superman costume he's wearing is the same one from the movie."

Still a bit dumbfounded, I glanced at Angie and whispered, "Christopher Reeve is standing in Brian's bedroom."

"Come on over here." Brian waved, heading toward the door. "I have something else to show you."

Our little group followed him to another room.

"Do you know the name of the first book ever printed on the Gutenberg printing press?" Brian asked.

Someone in our group responded, "The Bible?"

"Yes, that's right. Would you like to see a page from the very first Bible ever printed?"

We swarmed over to where he was standing. Sure enough, there it was: Acts chapter 20 from the Gutenberg Bible.

Between Johnny Cash, Superman, and a page from the first mass-produced work from a printing press, my night had already been made. Just when I thought things couldn't get better, however,

Brian handed me an old, tattered book. "It's a hymnal from the 1800s, the first to contain the greatest hymn ever written, 'Amazing Grace.'"

My eye started twitching.

"Do you know what it's called?" Brian asked, testing my knowledge.

"Uhhh, the *Olney Hymns*?" My voice was shaky not from a lack of confidence in the answer but from the shock of actually holding in my hands the book I had recently heard about.

"You're right!" Brian replied, his eyebrows raising slightly as if he was casually impressed.

"I visited Olney this summer and am currently writing about the lives of Newton and Cowper!" I volunteered.

"Nice! Well, then you probably know about C. S. Lewis and J. R. R. Tolkien."

"Y-yes!" I stammered. "I'm writing about them too!"

"Then you might be interested in looking through some of their personal correspondence."

"You have actual letters penned by Lewis and Tolkien?"

"Oh, sure. Hold on." Brian rummaged around in a nearby desk and handed me a large book. "Here you go."

Mentally drifting from the rest of the group and forgetting for a time where I was, I immersed myself in the penmanship of two of the world's greatest fantasy writers.

Brian came close, drawing me out of my drunken literary stupor. "Since you seem interested in these English authors, you may have heard of George MacDonald."

At this point I looked around for Ashton Kutcher and a hidden camera. No way was this real.

"You know," my new friend began, beckoning me over to the side of the room, "it's a shame most pastors can't afford some of these special books. They're the ones who would probably appreciate them most." Brian pressed another book into my hand and said, "Here. I want you to have this."

I was at a loss for words when my eyes fell on the title.

Phantastes by George MacDonald.

Brian pointed to the iconic work. "You know the significance of this book? It impacted Lewis in a big way. It's a first edition. You can have it."

I couldn't contain my smile.

And I thought I might need a clean pair of shorts.

Stunned, I mumbled incoherently through a deeply grateful thank-you and then backed myself into a corner, clutching the now-most-significant book I own as if it were a small animal rescued from the flames. My wife had often asked me about my preferred love language. It became clear in that moment that it's collectible books.

The night didn't end there. It went on like this for a while, our group repeatedly mesmerized as Brian and Sally continued displaying their fascinating collection of relics. We were treated to famous paintings, old manuscripts, ancient artifacts, and a plethora of Bibles.

Before the night came to an end, Brian showed us a large blue box. "I told you I grew up in Japan, right? Well, I met a guy there whose father was an architect. When his father died, he left him many of his architectural drawings. The fellow didn't want them and put them up for auction. Knowing that these blueprints may be some of the few in existence, I bid right away and ..." His voice trailed off as he uncovered what was inside.

I promise I am not making this up. Right in front of us, Brian disclosed the blueprints to the World Trade Center. Both towers.

Our film director, Zach, who had joined us for this party, exclaimed in disbelief over my shoulder, "Where *are* we right now?"

Brian and Sally were such a delight. Brian's passion for sharing the hope of Jesus through artifacts and storytelling was almost overwhelming.

Sally's quiet strength and determination to see the vision through sparked in us an instant admiration.

The playfulness of the evening was reminiscent of what I had read about life in the MacDonald house. Their house, like this one, seemed to be full of love, laughter, entertainment, and a deep desire to demonstrate the artful glory of God.

LEAVING ENGLAND

After filming in Hyde Park, our team gathered our belongings, careful not to end the moment too soon. Our reflections on the life of George MacDonald had left us introspective. As we walked away, we discussed how thankful we were for people like MacDonald, whose writings were a deep well to which we could repeatedly return to find refreshment.

With darkness descending, we made our way toward the train that would carry us through the fifty-and-a-half-kilometer Chunnel under the English Channel to our next destination, Pas-de-Calais, France. As we boarded the train, we chattered excitedly about our time in England and how blessed we all felt to be included in God's divine love story. For some reason, certainly beyond anything we could comprehend, God was allowing us to have this experience.

And rather than analyze it, we were simply living it the best we knew how. Following the example of this inspired English poet, we embraced and enjoyed "the holy moment."

Chapter 5

OUR HEARTS ARE MADE FOR LOVE

Saint Thérèse of Lisieux, AD 1873–1897, Normandy, France

How perfectly our hearts are made for love.

"You Are Love & Love Alone," All Sons & Daughters

My friend Terri, a rancher and equine instructor, stopped by to see me one day. She has lent me a little room that sits at the edge of one of her stables in the rolling countryside of Arrington, Tennessee. Looking out my window, I can see the leaves giving up their resistance to turn. In the pasture, two horses graze aimlessly. Occasionally they look my way, and their energy invites me to be content. A casual step, a flick of the tail, a mouthful of grass—ahh, if only I could exist with that kind of simplicity.

"How's it going?" Terri asked, walking toward the door.

I told her I was just getting down to business, about to enter the story of Saint Thérèse of Lisieux.

"She's different from Mother Teresa, right?"

"Right. Saint Thérèse was a French nun who found joy in the little things. Sadly she died when she was very young."

"That's so crazy," my friend responded. "The other day I was reading about how our names affect our destinies. And while doing a Google search for 'Terri,' I kept coming across the name Saint Thérèse. I had never heard of her before, but I got curious about her story."

"What did you discover?"

"Not much," Terri said with a wry grin. "I wish someone would write about her—and the other saints, for that matter. With my Protestant upbringing, I don't know much about any of their stories."

FINDING HER IDENTITY

Born on January 2, 1873, near Normandy, France, Thérèse Martin was a precocious and energetic child, whose family enthusiastically cherished her.

Having suffered a deep and painful loss at the age of four when her mother died of breast cancer, Thérèse later wrote that the first part of her life stopped that day. She had been very close to her mom and longed for a matronly figure to fill those shoes. As a result, she clung to her older sister, Pauline, who would remain a mentoring presence throughout Thérèse's life. Following the tragic death of his wife, Thérèse's father, Louis, moved the family about sixty miles north to the little town of Lisieux so his children could be close to their mother's relatives.

Though an earnest zeal for God and a knowledge of the catechism of the Catholic Church filled Thérèse's youth, a great deal of pain also characterized these years of her life. She suffered severely from headaches and bouts of insomnia. Her condition baffled doctors, and they offered no relief.

At one point Thérèse was diagnosed with scruples, a psychological illness likened to obsessive-compulsive disorder and marked by pathological guilt about moral and religious issues. She was constantly preoccupied with a fear of sinning, which caused her to weep often. She also had a profound sense of empathy and a deep longing for approval. Her hypersensitivity to what others thought about her combined with her fear of disappointing God led her to feel despondent and, at times, inconsolable.

At ten years of age, Thérèse had such an intense mental and physical breakdown that she began hallucinating. Once, when her father walked into her bedroom to check on her, she noticed the hat he was holding in his hands and began to shriek at the top of her lungs, imagining he was standing over her holding a menacing object. Louis left the room in tears. With no success treating her condition medically, in great desperation Thérèse and her family continued to pray fervently.

One day lying in bed and praying for a cure, Thérèse looked over at a statue of the Virgin Mary. It appeared as if the figure came alive and smiled at her. In that moment the illness subsided.

Three years later on Christmas Eve in 1886, Thérèse experienced what she called her complete conversion. That day in a final surrender to God, she found a new confidence in her identity in Him. Her questions, her doubts, and her fears faded away.

At a young age, Thérèse cultivated what many fail to develop in a lifetime: *resilience*.

Ronald Rolheiser observes, "Much good is happening in therapeutic rooms and in growth groups today as we get in touch with our wounds, addictions, and dysfunctions.... But there is also the tendency among too many of us to let the therapy itself and the new sensitivity become yet another addiction. When this happens, then sensitivity to our wounds and dysfunctions tends to make us so oversensitive that we become impossible to live with because everything hurts us so badly."[1]

God was shaping in Thérèse an inner strength that would thrust her into young adulthood and give her confidence beyond her years.

Propelled by her profound religious experiences, Thérèse hoped to follow in the footsteps of her beloved sister Pauline, who became a

Carmelite nun. At fifteen Thérèse, accompanied by her father, presented herself to the local bishop for acceptance to the convent. The bishop told her she would be considered; however, because she was so young, she would probably have to wait a few years. In the absence of a sincere commitment from her local religious authority, Thérèse made up her mind to ask the pope himself.

Happy to oblige his daughter, Louis made arrangements for a trip to Rome that included both Thérèse and her sister Celine. The history of Rome instantly captivated Thérèse. The thoughts of Christian martyrs, their sacrifice, and their courage aroused within her a deep sense of awe and gratitude. Visiting the Colosseum, Thérèse and her sister ignored the posted prohibitions and, sneaking away from their group, explored the vast structure as far as the arena floor. Still audacious as ever, Thérèse was determined to make the most of her visit of a lifetime.

I can relate. Whenever I see a sign that says Keep Out, my curiosity is heightened, and I long to go in. Later on our trip, standing outside the Cathedral of Notre-Dame in Paris, I would have my opportunity.

When the day arrived for the family's audience before Pope Leo XIII, Thérèse, Louis, Celine, and others standing in line were given specific instructions: they were to listen but refrain from speaking to the Holy Father.

In spite of the warning, Thérèse ignored any sense of decorum and, seizing the moment, left her place in line and threw herself at the pope's feet, begging for entrance into the cloistered life of the convent. Because of her refusal to leave, the guards had to physically pick her up and carry her to the door, but not before she heard Leo's hopeful response: "Go—go—you will enter if God wills it."[2]

God willed it. On April 9, 1888, Thérèse was admitted into the Carmelite convent in Lisieux. What she had longed for "since the dawn of reason,"[3] as she put it, had finally become a reality.

THE LITTLE WAY

Perhaps it was from receiving an abundance of love at home that Thérèse, at such an early age, was able to give her attention to loving God and those in need. Having lost four of their nine children to tragic deaths at young ages, her parents poured their affection into their remaining five daughters. After their mother died, Thérèse's sisters, each in succession, mothered the little girl with utmost devotion. Having such a love modeled for her seemed to form in Thérèse a deep reservoir of love and a great capacity to live a love-filled life.

For better or worse, our experiences with our parents often shape our view of God. If we view Him as a whimsical being who doesn't set boundaries or limits, we may expect Him to give us everything we ask for and then find ourselves disappointed when He doesn't. If we understand Him to be a condemning, unapproachable tyrant, we may avoid spending time in conversation with Him. We need God's Word and the Holy Spirit to constantly reveal who and what kind of God He is so that we can respond in truth.

Like George MacDonald, Thérèse had an unshakable confidence in God's love. She never seemed to falter in her recognition of God as a loving father of His children.

Let the little children come to me, and do not hinder them,
for the kingdom of heaven belongs to such as these.[4]

Jesus

A year before she entered the convent, Thérèse experienced a moment of grace that affected her for the rest of her life. She overheard her father say something about her that wasn't nice. Instead of wallowing in hurt feelings and spiraling downward into self-pity and self-loathing, Thérèse shifted her thoughts toward how she could love him instead. With this intentional focus on love, she began living out what she would one day be known for: the "little way."

> I will seek out a means of getting to Heaven by a little way—very short and very straight, a little way that is wholly new. We live in an age of inventions; nowadays the rich need not trouble to climb the stairs, they have lifts instead. Well, I mean to try and find a lift by which I may be raised unto God, for I am too tiny to climb the steep stairway of perfection....
>
> Thine Arms, then, O Jesus, are the lift which must raise me up even unto Heaven. To get there I need not grow; on the contrary, I must remain little, I must become still less.[5]

Thérèse viewed the pathway to God's Kingdom not as a long list of heroic or grandiose achievements but rather as a simple expression of kindness. She wrote,

> Love proves itself by deeds, so how am I to show my love? Great deeds are forbidden me. The only way I can prove my love is by scattering flowers and these flowers are every little sacrifice, every glance and word, and the doing of the least actions for love.[6]

Thérèse searched for opportunities to live sacrificially. She was known for eating what was placed in front of her without complaining, regardless of how bland the food might be. She smiled at her Carmelite sisters, who were unkind to her. On one occasion she was blamed for knocking over a vase, and though she didn't do it, she asked for forgiveness and bore the humiliation. In radical divergence from her childhood, she was willing to be misunderstood, walk peacefully in grace, and allow time to reveal the truth.

John, the disciple of Jesus who was also known for his capacity to love, wrote this in a letter to the early church:

> This is how we've come to understand and experience love: Christ sacrificed his life for us. This is why we ought to live sacrificially for our fellow believers, and not just be out for ourselves. If you see some brother or sister in need and have the means to do something about it but turn a cold shoulder and do nothing,

what happens to God's love? It disappears. And you made it disappear.

My dear children, let's not just talk about love; let's practice real love. This is the only way we'll know we're living truly, living in God's reality. It's also the way to shut down debilitating self-criticism, even when there is something to it. For God is greater than our worried hearts and knows more about us than we do ourselves.[7]

Living with great restrictions as a nun and dying from tuberculosis at the age of twenty-four, Thérèse never had a chance to accomplish the deeds of greatness most historians herald. Yet her small acts of love have influenced generations of people around the world.

MONT-SAINT-MICHEL CASTLE

While our team wasn't able to visit the convent in Lisieux, we were able to tour an island citadel in northwestern France called Mont-Saint-Michel. Its history, which included a legend about the archangel Michael and an inspiring story about Joan of Arc, intrigued us, so we carved out some time to visit the iconic world heritage site.

As we got closer to this mountain in the sea, we couldn't spit out adjectives fast enough. True tourists, we paused every few feet for pictures and then continued in our attempt to put words to our fascination with the majestic city on a hill. Ashton pointed out, and it was hard to disagree, that Mont-Saint-Michel looked a lot like the castle from Disney's movie *Tangled*. We made our way into this French magical kingdom and walked the narrow streets crammed with endless restaurants, cafés, and shops. Getting our workout for the day, we ascended hundreds of steep steps until we arrived at the entrance to the grand ecclesiastical structure that crowns this royal bastion.

As the carefree breeze brushed past us, the shadows and brick provided cool corners of retreat from the warm sun. Cresting the final stair, we walked toward the edge of the parapet. The panoramic view once again left us with a sense of inadequacy. We finally gave up our attempts at associations and gazed in silence.

What we cannot comprehend in analysis,
we become aware of in awe.[8]

Abraham Joshua Heschel

Before the trip, my friend Jeremy let me borrow one of his cameras. This was more than a kind gesture, because he is one of the world's premiere photographers, and his camera was a nice one. Being a few notches below novice, I lacked a certain admiration for the fine instrument in my hand. After a little show-and-tell with our film director, Zach, I slowly began to appreciate how amazing the camera was and how proficient I wasn't. Without hesitation I asked for help, officially appointing myself Zach's apprentice. While this was probably not one of Zach's goals for the trip, he humored me and, with bountiful patience, repeatedly explained the functions of the fourteen thousand buttons and their derivatives.

Now a few days into the trip, a heroic confidence swept through me as I stood on the summit of this island fortress. I announced to the team that I was prepared to capture a shot of epic proportions. After herding everyone to the front of a ledge and going through what I deemed to be an impressive amount of eye squinting and squatting (imitating my photographer friends), I set up a fantastic shot. Actually, several fantastic shots. And man, I am telling you, they were good. Really good. Competition-worthy good.

Alas, my evaluation of my photographic profundity will never be confirmed, for when I handed the camera back to Zach, he looked down at it and, squinting into the sun with a half smile, said to me, "You forgot to take off the lens cap."

MADE FOR LOVE

After entering the large church building, we listened to a tour guide discuss some of the history of this medieval town.

The place felt cold. Spiritually. There was an absence of life.

As I half listened to the guide drone on and on, my mind drifted to Saint Thérèse. Her story was full of light and warmth. Most significantly, it was full.

What a contrast. An enormous, cold, empty church structure, and the life of the Little Flower, as Thérèse was known. She wasn't flamboyant. Or overwhelming.

She was unnoticed. Hidden.

Recognized only in her simple acts of love.

The apostle Paul wrote these words to a young church plant: "If I speak in the tongues of men or of angels, but do not have love, I am only a resounding gong or a clanging cymbal."[9]

If you've ever made the mistake of buying your child a toy that makes a recurring noise, you understand the metaphor.

Paul continued ...

"Love is patient,

"Love is kind.

"It does not envy....

"It does not dishonor others,

"It is not self-seeking,

"It is not easily angered,

"It keeps no record of wrongs.

"Love does not delight in evil."[10]

The contrast to love is lust. Unlike love, lust wants immediate gratification.

Lust is unkind.

Lust is jealous.

Lust is abrupt.

Lust is always me first.

Lust gets angry when it doesn't get what it wants.

Lust plays the victim card.

Lust finds its pleasure in what ends in shame.

Love, on the other hand, "rejoices with the truth."

It protects.

It trusts.

It hopes.

It perseveres.

"Love never fails."[11]

My wife recently started sending me simple texts to celebrate something good once a day in our lives. These texts have been like little flowers. Acts of love long remembered.

In the garden of Eden, the serpent lied to God's human creatures about love and tempted them with what was taboo: "The appeal to Eve's senses comes with a promise that the fruit will deliver something it can't—specifically, a better reality than the one God has made. The problem isn't the fruit. It's what is promised through the fruit—that she won't die if she eats it.... "Lust promises what it can't deliver."[12]

The tempter was essentially saying, "Look, I'm suggesting a better way, because the truth is, God is holding out on you."

When we act out of lust, we give in to this lie. How do we know when we've caved to this temptation? On the back end of lustful behavior, we're left with nothing but a failed promise. And usually with a number of other consequences as well.

Contrast this with Thérèse's belief that if one commits small acts of love, the end result is a blessed life.

Lust always tries to counterfeit love. And lust ultimately comes from a deep dissatisfaction with life.

When we struggle with lust, we lack internal peace. We're looking for something, searching for someone. We're dissatisfied.

How do we counter dissatisfaction?

Gratitude.

And as Thérèse so eloquently wrote, "I realised thoroughly that joy is not found in the things which surround us, but lives only in the soul. One could possess it as well in an obscure prison as in the palace of a king."[13]

Thérèse of the Holy Face, as she was also called, often expressed this spirit of gratitude when taking Communion. For her, remembering the sufferings of Christ was a catalyst to her unbridled enthusiasm for what that suffering had provided her: eternal abundance in heaven with the King.

When we partake in Communion by breaking bread (symbolizing Christ's body) and drinking the fruit of the vine (symbolizing His blood), we remember the great sacrifice of Jesus, the Son of God. In this remembrance, we're roused into a spirit of gratitude. And in that moment, we reconsider what in life is of greatest value.

God's Son died to pay for our sins. He was then raised to life, crushing death and making a way for us to live out eternal life. Should we choose to receive this gift, we become blessed. And in this blessing, we can't help but be thankful.

This is one of the many reasons we're called to remember the Lord's Supper.

Every time we're reminded of the goodness of God, we dispel the darkness of dissatisfaction. If we don't fill our lives with the light of thankfulness and joy, the dark world is more than willing to offer us temporary solutions to relieve our disillusionment with life.

THE GOAL OF LOVE

The ultimate goal of love is connection. When you read the Bible, read it in that light. The entire book is a social history. While it may include rules and regulations, they were never the point. They were meant to direct us to Someone.

Moral integrity is an expression of connectedness.

Lust wants to pull us away from relationship. Love wants to pull us into it. The entire Bible is full of contrasts between connectedness and disconnectedness.

People suffer to the extent that they are removed from the truth.
People are healed to the extent that they embrace it.[14]
Dr. Keith Ablow

When Jesus Christ died on the cross, He took upon Himself my lust and yours. All of it. Even the lust that is yet to come. He paid the price so that you and I don't have to walk out lives of shame and condemnation. Should we choose to receive it, forgiveness is available to each of us.

Thérèse wrote, "[God] wishes me to love Him, because He has forgiven me, not much, but everything."[15] The love of God, like morning sunshine on our pillows, awakens us to new life. This love knows no bounds. It's not contingent on our ability to suffer profusely, withstand sin, or please others. God's ineffable, steadfast love permeates our misunderstandings, washes away our sin, and redeems our souls.

OMAHA BEACH

After we had concluded our time at Mont-Saint-Michel, Chris walked up and said, "The bus driver wants to know if there is anyplace we would like to go, as we have some time to kill before driving to Paris."

I responded immediately, "Omaha Beach!"

Reviewing a map, Ashton determined that we were just a few hours away. The driver was confident he could get us there close to midnight. We decided to go for it.

Arriving at the beach in the final moments of twilight, we disembarked with a quiet reverence for a place where so many souls had been taken prematurely from the planet. I've been an avid student of World War II history since I first pulled an issue of *LIFE* magazine from the shelf of the Clearfield Library in Williamsville, New York, when I was twelve. Standing on Omaha Beach while orange-and-pink rays of light danced along the horizon was and is one of the most memorable moments of my life.

As if that weren't enough, David, Leslie, and Cara pulled out their instruments and, with Zach's camera rolling, began singing their song "Great Are You Lord."

I kneeled in the sand. I prayed. I cried.

And I felt within me an overwhelming sense of gratitude for a generation of men and women who paid the ultimate sacrifice for my freedom. I thought about my nineteen-year-old sons and how it could have been them lying in the surf, dismembered and lifeless. I could have been the father who lost his boys.

My prayer went something like this:

> *Dear God. I am looking out over a beach where fathers of nineteen-year-old boys lost their sons. Those boys gave up their lives for a cause much greater than they could comprehend. They gave up their lives for freedom. They fought a great evil in the world and paid the ultimate sacrifice.*
>
> *Father, show me my enemy so that I would be bold, direct, and fearless. So that I would have a fierce intentionality.*
>
> *How am I meant to bring my one tiny, precious life to bear on this planet? How am I meant to stem the tide of evil? What must I surrender?*

Show me my purpose.

Thérèse gave up her freedoms for a life dedicated to prayer. It seems that for poets and saints, love doesn't exist without some form of sacrifice. Kneeling and praying on the beach that night, I was slowly beginning to accept that anything of value comes with a cost.

THE VOICE OF ARCHITECTURE

Paris, France

With a day off in Paris, Ashton and I did our best to absorb the City of Light. We strolled along the Seine River, our eyes glancing back and forth from the exquisite architecture patiently awaiting an audience to the expectant voyagers rubbernecking their way through the city. Each statue, figure, building, and tower seemed to lean inward, inviting us to behold their stories of stone.

Our next stop was Versailles. After a Frenchwoman showed me to a back room where we could buy tickets from a machine instead of lingering in a forty-five-minute line, we joined the other tourists and entered one of the world's most legendary royal palaces. Following the herd, Ashton and I gazed upon the baroque architecture, pausing on occasion to look toward the skies. The painted ones. With naked people.

We meandered through endless rooms splashed in gold and reviewed painting after painting of famous French people. After spending time with the many kings named Louis, we strolled through the gardens and discussed the opulence. The wealth surrounding us was difficult to digest. I found myself longing for heaven, thankful for the nature and reign of a different kind of king.

Boarding the train back to Paris, I handed Ashton a map and said, "Here you go, Captain. You get to plot our course again."

"What?" she exclaimed, a slight shadow of fear cast over her face. "I already did that in London, Dad! You didn't say anything about French cities!"

I smiled. "Ashton, I know you're most confident when you have time to prepare. But life throws us curveballs, and sometimes you have to figure things out as you go. Your life lesson for today: do hard things."

It was a quiet train ride.

Ashton gathered her courage and navigated our way through the city to the Eiffel Tower. At the top of Paris's famed structure, the city sprawling in every direction, we took in the panorama.

I looked at my daughter as she gazed down at the city.

She was smiling.

I was smiling.

My view was better than hers.

From the time Ashton was a child with blonde-streaked hair, people have always told her how pretty she is. Age has only crystallized that belief. Though I couldn't have framed the words at the time, what I saw as the memories splashed over her was more than a beautiful, young woman. There before me was a soul taking flight. My child was finding her wings. And somehow I knew that her kindness and bravery were going to leave the world she encountered a better place.

In that moment, standing on a tower over Paris, I was reminded what a blessing it is to be a father.

Paris was as magical as we had hoped it would be, and so it was with progressive sadness that I took Ashton to the airport early the next morning for her flight home. As you might imagine, I had a degree of trepidation. But this was her final test. And this time I made sure she was fully hydrated.

I arrived at the airport feeling forlorn yet enthusiastic, for while I was sending my daughter back home, I was also picking up my twin nineteen-year-old sons. I had arranged for the boys to join our trip as a way for them to connect with their European fans, hang out with their dad, and help our film crew with the gear. As the two came into my line of sight, I noticed quickly that Tyler was walking like a zombie and looked close to death. Jordan looked only slightly less dead. It turns out they had both come down with colds just before leaving home, and neither of them slept on their overnight flight.

When we arrived at our hotel, within minutes Tyler was curled up in bed, where he would remain for the next twenty-two hours.

Feeling a bit better, and not wanting to miss out on Paris, Jordan accompanied me to meet the team near the great Cathedral of Notre-Dame for our next film segment. We arrived to find the line so long that I was concerned we would miss our filming. Looking for alternative solutions, we found a random gate with a door and surprisingly discovered it was ajar.

Jordan looked at me with an easier-to-ask-for-forgiveness-than-permission look.

We entered and moseyed along an interior garden to a side entrance of the cathedral. Jordan walked up the stone steps and peered inside the first cathedral he had ever seen. His jaw dropped, and in astonishment, "Oh, my word!" and "Dad, this is incredible!" tumbled from his mouth.

Staring at the stained-glass kaleidoscope on the west portal, we were both mesmerized. The detail, the symmetry, the craftsmanship, the vision—Notre-Dame is inspiring with or without the hunchback. After joining in with my own superlatives about how the art and architecture made me feel both small and sublime, I imagined what it must have been like eight hundred years ago when this beacon of hope dominated the landscape for miles in every direction.

When we finally connected with the team, David, Cara, Sarah, and I filmed a piece about the voice of architecture, something we've had a great deal of discussion about and whose seminal interests sparked this epic journey.

THE LANGUAGE OF BEAUTY

French philosopher Alain de Botton wrote, "In the eyes of medieval man, a cathedral was God's house on earth."[1]

Sarah wondered aloud ...

"Does God need our words in order to be revealed?

"Or does He also whisper through a brushstroke? In a melody? In carefully arranged and colored glass? In something we can't explain, something that takes our breath away?

"Does He speak through what is simply beautiful?"

Motioning with his hand toward the cathedral, David posed another question: "Why are we drawn to these grand accomplishments?" After pausing he continued: "I think it's because they are so much bigger than any one person. There's no way I could build this on my own."

The rest of us agreed. When we looked at a cathedral like Notre-Dame, it prompted us to consider what thing of beauty we might create if we drew in our focus, worked diligently, took the long view, and collaborated charitably with others.

That kind of dreaming is scary. That kind of risk is unnerving. And there, along the underbelly of our visions, lies an unspoken reality.

Sometimes we believe we're better off without beauty.

Think about it. Aren't there times you don't want to recall sweet memories?

Ever had a moment when you pulled your gaze from a sunset or mountain vista because deep inside you knew the view would come to an end anyway, and in the agony of it all, you decided there would be less pain if you determined the ending rather than letting the ending sneak up on you?

I wonder how many relationships have ended for this very reason.

Beauty is wild. Intimidating. Glorious. It reminds us of the great beyond.

That makes us feel sad. And sometimes, that sadness is too much to bear.

This strange dichotomy is captured delightfully in Disney Pixar's film *Inside Out*.[2] In this animated frolic, the emotions of a girl named Riley are personified through characters with the same names—joy, anger, sadness, fear, and disgust. The writers magnificently captured the theme that joy and sadness must coexist. Without their important alliance, Riley would fail to understand that life has deep meaning.

According to Alain de Botton,

> A perplexing consequence of fixing our eyes on an ideal is that it may make us sad. The more beautiful something is, the sadder we risk feeling....
>
> Our sadness won't be of the searing kind but more like a blend of joy and melancholy: joy at the perfection we see before us, melancholy at an awareness of how seldom we are sufficiently blessed to encounter anything of its kind. The flawless object throws into perspective the mediocrity that surrounds it. We are reminded of the way we would wish things always to be and of how incomplete our lives remain.[3]

Sometimes in the Western church, there's a tendency to use hype as a mechanism for minimization and denial. If we can get pumped up enough, we can forget at least temporarily that life is hard, that we have doubts, that we struggle with sin, and that we're a far cry from Eden. In some circles there's no room for lament. No space for sorrow.

If we purpose in our hearts to never experience melancholy, we'll miss out on a great deal of beauty.

Blessed are those who mourn,
for they will be comforted.[4]

Jesus

In this life we cannot deny the incompleteness we feel. God knows this and, in His creative pursuit, beckons us to stop, look, and listen. He uses more than just words to move our hearts and draw us to Himself. He speaks to us through images, icons, curves, and colors. Of course, like anything else, His communication to us can be twisted and misaligned. The medium of art can become an end in itself, and wood and stone can take on the forms of gods. Our fallen nature is unflinching in its determination to find shortcuts to worship.

For this reason, a young Frenchman, among others, found himself thrust to the forefront of the religious world's understanding of worship and interpretation of Scripture.

His name was John Calvin.

Chapter 6

THE PERSONAL GOD

John Calvin, AD 1509–1564, Geneva, Switzerland

In every nation on the earth this song of ours is rising.
"Creation Sings," All Sons & Daughters

The following morning, having slept for most of the day and night, Tyler revived. Feeling energetic, he walked toward the twin doors of our hotel-room balcony, flung them wide open, and said, "Wow, Paris looks like an amazing city!"

Jordan and I smiled.

"Yeah, hope you liked it," Jordan chided. "Time to get on the bus for Switzerland."

During the ride, a handful of us started discussing the man who has been both villain and hero to many. Born sixty miles northeast of Paris in 1509 and schooled in both law and theology, John Calvin is known today as one of history's great Reformers of the Protestant faith. In many ways, this Frenchman's beliefs and logical persuasions were responsible for much of our American way of life. His "legacy has been traced in everything from modern marriage and modern science to modern liberal government and of course modern capitalism. By many accounts, he is a major source of modernity's very understanding of the self."[1]

In his Ecclesiastical Ordinances, Calvin organized the ministry of the church into four different branches of government and administration. Distancing himself from the absolute authority modeled in monarchy and the papacy, he used the New Testament's example of organization as a model for checks and balances of power. Calvin's doctrine influenced not only the church and its leadership but also civil government. "It was Founding Father and the second President of the United States, John Adams, who described Calvin as 'a vast genius,' a man of 'singular eloquence, vast erudition, and polished taste, [who] embraced the cause of Reformation,' adding: 'Let not Geneva be forgotten or despised. Religious liberty owes it much respect.'"[2]

When we think about the land of the free and the home of the brave, we sometimes forget what it took for us to become an independent nation. A friend of mine, Joel, sings with a band he formed with his brother. They are from Australia. We were watching the Super Bowl together one year, and Joel was so moved by the singing of our national anthem that he had tears in his eyes. His wife and those of us sitting nearby chuckled as Joel remarked, "You Americans and your love for your country!"

As far as nations go, the United States of America is still quite young, and many of our citizens have staved off the cynicism that those in older nations tend to have. I admit I still get a lump in my throat at times when our flag is raised and our values are reaffirmed.

THE YOUNG ACTIVIST

In his twenties, John Calvin split from the Roman Catholic Church and began teaching and writing about his bold, nonconformist views in the French capital. Forced to flee Paris for his progressive beliefs, Calvin relocated to Basel, Switzerland, and in 1536, published the first edition of his controversial magnum opus on Reformed Protestant theology, *Institutes of the Christian Religion*.

Calvin, self-described as antisocial and shy, wanted to avoid getting involved in the public game. He had no desire to be a leader in this religious movement but rather sought to live in a quiet place where he could think and continue to write doctrine around the Reformed thoughts that were emerging among those who rebelled against contemporary Catholicism.

Calvin left Basel, intending to move to Strasbourg, Germany, a place where the Protestant movement was strong and literary activity was bright. On his way he accepted an invitation to spend a day in Geneva, Switzerland. While he was there, a fiery Reformer by the name of William Farel searched out Calvin. With Calvin's popularity swelling since *Institutes* was published, Farel saw in him a man who could unite the religious revolutionaries and put words to what they were feeling.

The new Protestant movement desperately needed to know what they were for, not just what they were against. So when Farel found Calvin in the Swiss city, he cornered him and listed a litany of reasons why it was important for Calvin to stay in Geneva and leverage his influence.

Calvin wasn't interested. He wanted to write in peace away from the friction of religious intolerance. Farel was frustrated with Calvin's desire for comfort and serenity. He needed a man who had the credibility to lead and was convinced Calvin was that man. Whether it was Holy Spirit zeal or desperate manipulation, Farel boldly told Calvin, "May God condemn your repose, and the calm you seek for study, if before such a great need you withdraw, and refuse your succor and help."[3]

Farel's rebuke convicted Calvin. He chose to stay put in Geneva and eventually became the pastor at Saint Peter's Cathedral. He continued teaching and collaborating on morality decrees, while shaping church government, and writing and creating new editions of the original *Institutes*, which was becoming—and which many still consider today—*the* apologetic for Protestantism. Calvin shook things up concerning many different aspects of Christian theology, including his views on the sacraments, predestination, and the absolute sovereignty of God. His views are still debated vehemently in college dorm rooms and church vestibules around the world.

When I heard of Calvin's desire to escape from the pressures of church leadership to write a theological treatise while in seclusion, I understood.

Recently I was talking with my friend Darren, a local pastor. He told me about a conversation he'd had with another pastor from Colorado. Darren's friend said that although all was well and his church was growing and healthy, he kept fantasizing about escaping, sneaking off in the middle of the night, running from the pressure and responsibility of being a pastor. I shifted in my seat, not saying a word as Darren continued talking.

Finally I confessed, "Man, it's so good to know that I'm not alone."

I love our church. Our people are kind and compassionate, vulnerable, and adventurous.

I'm not worn out by their demands. I'm worn out from my own.

I'm coming to understand that in any job, one can fulfill only so many roles. When I try to do it all, I get stretched, and sadly I've come all too close to being completely broken. I wrote in my first book, *Love Well*, that I've always had trouble with boundaries. I'm still very much on a journey of learning how to say no and when to say yes. The delicate balance as a pastor—and this also seems to be true as a parent—is between making healthy choices regarding appropriate tasks and activities to delegate and being confident in what I must give my direct attention.

Just because I can doesn't mean I should.

I've come to understand, and research for this book has reminded me, that there is no one-size-fits-all template. No poet, saint, pastor, or parent does it exactly the same way. And we aren't meant to.

Life is a dance with the Spirit.

Will we lead or will we follow?

Calvin felt the Spirit impressing him to stay in Geneva. By choosing to remain, he was given an opportunity to consider his theology through the lens of real people in real time.

SAINT PETER'S CATHEDRAL

After our team arrived in Geneva, it took us a bit of time to locate Calvin's church. Few Swiss seemed confident of its location, if they knew of the church at all.

After about twenty-five minutes wandering the charming streets of the old city, we turned a corner, and there before us was the cathedral. This building where Calvin's church met was quite the contrast to Notre-Dame. Though large and cavernous, Saint Peter's offered a serene simplicity. Before long someone had discovered a way to the top of the building, where we could walk through the bell towers to an exterior balcony. Our group made the ascent.

As we walked out onto the terrace, a breathtaking view greeted us. Below us lay a patchwork of terra-cotta, tile rooftops. Ahead of us on the horizon lay the Swiss Alps plunging into the waters of Lake Geneva. A fountain of white water sprayed effortlessly upward from the edge of the lake, setting itself against a backdrop of vibrant blue and green.

I wondered aloud how often Calvin came up here to take in the view. Was he romanced by beauty? How did he feel when he looked out over a city in conflict? What motivated him as he shaped his expectations for how followers of Jesus should represent their savior? At the intersection of creation's elegance and the pain of humanity, did he determine in his heart to write, sing, and pastor with a furious commitment to excellence?

What is less known is that Calvin was very influential in how Christians worshipped. He wrote, "A good affection toward God is not a thing dead and brutish, but a lively movement, proceeding from the Holy Spirit when the heart is rightly touched and the understanding is enlightened."[4]

Living in Music City, surrounded by professional musicians, I've found the musical worship experience at the forefront of many conversations. How do we serve God with excellence while not allowing what we produce to become an entertaining end in itself? How do we offer up our artistic expressions for inspiration rather than consumption?

We haven't resolved these questions, but we're recognizing that we avoid the personal presence of God when we focus our dialogue on utopian, abstract theological assumptions. It's easy to be an armchair worship theorist when you aren't the one who has to show up every week and guide distracted Westerners into the presence of God.

The Reformers, in their zeal for knowledge, sometimes drifted away from reality. When we get obsessive about defining our truths, we can get distracted and stop giving our attention to the Way, the Truth, and the Life.

Larry Crabb writes,

> When we value scholarly precision and doctrinal purity above a personally transforming encounter with the God who reveals himself in his Word, when we fail to see that an academic grasp of Scripture often leads to a proud appreciation of knowledge more than a humble and passionate appreciation of Christ, we develop an orthodoxy that crushes life. And we miss the gospel that frees us to live.[5]

MORE THAN A PHILOSOPHY

Of all the poets and saints I've researched, Calvin seems to elicit extreme emotions not only from his admirers but also from his detractors. He is both revered and reviled. As we consider his life, I must point out that we are each a work in progress. Calvin was no exception.

"Every follower of Jesus is a rough draft. Over time, the great Editor—the Holy Spirit—shapes our lives and views.... This is also true for those Christians who have gone before us. Therefore, one of the mistakes that we must guard against is to dismiss a person's entire contribution because they may hold (or have held) to ideas that we find hard to stomach."[6]

There is no question that had we worked alongside Calvin, we would have found some of his means and methods difficult to digest. Though powerful and influential in his ideas, Calvin had issues. For one, he was unruly and crass in his language toward those who disagreed with him. In Geneva, he enforced harsh and sometimes violent behavioral expectations that were not biblical—they were simply preferential to him and his tribe. If anyone showed up late to a worship service and entered after the sermon had begun, he or she would be admonished directly. If it happened again, that person would be fined. (Churchgoers in Nashville would be broke.) Adultery, blasphemy, idolatry, and heresy were punishable by death. "Calvin's own step-daughter and son-in-law were among those condemned for adultery and executed."[7]

Calvin's lowest moment, at least historically, was his involvement in the burning of accused heretic Michael Servetus. Servetus was a Spanish physician whose theological tenants and psychological teachings had offended the Catholic Church. The Catholic Inquisition had imprisoned him in France, but he escaped and was later recaptured in Geneva. Calvin, along with other Protestant leaders in Switzerland, agreed with the Catholics that Servetus was a heretic, and though Calvin proposed a more lenient punishment, he stood by as Servetus was burned at the stake. Understandably, Calvin was criticized for his involvement in the execution.

God does not impose truth from without. The truth of God
is not an alien invasion but a loving courtship.[8]

Eugene Peterson

The tragedy is that many of us spend our lifetimes pursuing a moral system while missing out on a personal interaction with Jesus. We chase after abstract beliefs, ethereal philosophies, and academic symposiums to debate. Many refuse to even consider alternative ideas unless certain words are used and sequenced in an exact rational and logical formula.

We tend to present Christianity, however unintentionally, as a competing ideological system, as if Christianity is a plastic duck bobbing alongside the other ducks of Hinduism, communism, or Buddhism, waiting to be plucked out of a pool at the fair.

We forget that Jesus came to earth not as a philosophy but as a baby.

Born to an unmarried teenager, who gave birth while retaining her virginity.

God born to humanity in innocence.

Asleep in an animal trough.

The Sovereign Presence here among us.

I think in our sin nature, we have an aversion to the manger. It's too simple. We want to make the work of salvation much more complex. The flesh always seeks out control. It's amazing how love can get lost in our efforts to morally organize our own lives and the lives of others. We work hard to build logical arguments, ironclad apologetics, and legal systems that, articulately fashioned, may win people over to our set of beliefs.

The pen is mightier than the sword. But is the pen mightier than an act of love?

You know what's interesting about our tendency to create religious systems? God has already revealed their futility. He designed such a structure for the Hebrew people—the Law. He offered this structure to reveal a universal human truth: apart from the Divine, humans will never get it right.

Humanity needed help—a rescuer, a restorer. So God incarnated Himself.

Rather than a religious system, He brought good news. This was the message of the angels to the shepherds the night Jesus came to the earth:

"I bring you good news that will cause great joy for all the people. Today in the town of David a Savior has been born to you; he is the Messiah, the Lord. This will be a sign to you: You will find a baby wrapped in cloths and lying in a manger."[9]

This amazing dispatch wasn't a set of abstract thoughts for these herdsmen to discuss over a good pipe and a campfire. It was a proclamation of hope embodied in human flesh. Hope experienced in a real live human being. One wrapped in cloths, resting in his exhausted father's arms, his mother's blood still stained on his skin.

It seems to me that the drama surrounding the birth of Christ is a continuous message of love and humility. The manger is a reminder.

God came to the earth.

The Divine took the form of a man.

He was slaughtered on a cross.

He died. Was buried. Rose again.

He ascended into heaven.

God endured the violence, the brokenness, and the frustration of this world. And He remains in an eternal love relationship with humanity. This story isn't about mankind but about a being named God.

I was struck by a tale I came across in a book by Eugene Peterson.[10] Father Tony Byrnne, a Jesuit missionary, tells of his experience with African villagers and their love for stories. Tony explained that the story of God was so compelling that his team of missionaries could hardly manage all the conversions. In an attempt to accelerate the maturity of his team, he would identify the brightest of the villagers and send them for Bible training in New York, Boston, Rome, or Dublin. After a few years of schooling, they would return to help with the spiritual formation of their peers.

The returning Bible teachers, however, weren't well received. When Tony inquired about the intense resistance these new instructors encountered, the villagers explained.

Their peers no longer told stories.

They taught doctrines, drew diagrams, and gave directions. "The intimate and dignifying process of telling a parable had been sold for a mess of academic pottage."[11]

Concluding his story, Father Byrnne shared that he no longer sends his young, intelligent converts off to "storyless schools."

Oh, how we get preoccupied with learning for the sake of being right. It's tempting to spend inordinate amounts of energy on the politics of humanity and forget Calvin's most basic premise, which he seemed to have forgotten at times too: humankind exists under the umbrella of the sovereignty of God.

CALVIN'S LEGACY

As our team looked out over the crystalline waters of Lake Geneva, we considered Calvin's life. While his methods and hypervigilance drifted toward moralism, his impact on the history of the church and political structures for governing humanity cannot be dismissed. Regardless of his severe methods, Calvin's motives seem to be clear: he desired to unite the Reformers under one banner of doctrine, depose monarchs of absolute authority in both church and state, and formulate a standard of holiness through intense subjugation of what he would have considered the pleasures of this world.

We have in Calvin a man limited by his context but passionate and effective in his ability to reform and unite a culture in chaos.

I often wonder how we'll be remembered years from now. When people look back at the church of the twenty-first century, what will they say?

I suppose what is most important is that we take responsibility for ourselves. And so with great conviction, I grasp tightly to this ancient scripture: "As for me and my household, we will serve the LORD."[12]

Chapter 7

CREATED FOR MORE

Saint Augustine of Hippo, AD 354–430, Milan, Italy

Our hearts are restless until they find rest in you.

"Rest in You," All Sons & Daughters

After climbing out of my coffin-sized bunk and maneuvering down the stairs of our bus to the lounge area, I made myself a shake and plopped onto the leather couch next to Cara and Leslie, who were already up reading, chatting, and sipping coffee. I looked out the windows and sighed. Below the bursts of orange and gold that stretched lazily across the morning sky, the Italian countryside bobbed by us like emerald waves against an endless horizon.

We finally made our way into the crowded streets on the outskirts of Milan and parked our bus at a hotel. Jordan and Tyler went on ahead of the group. They were eager to get into the city, since they had planned to visit with some of their most dedicated Italian fans.

Before filming our first segment in front of the small Basilica di Sant'Ambrogio, I made plans to eat lunch with the boys, arranging to meet them at the Piazza del Duomo, Milan's central square. The Milan Cathedral, or the Duomo, one of the largest cathedrals in all of Italy, dominates the plaza like a Gothic guardian over the city. The sun blazing above, I strolled through a swarm of attentive pigeons collecting at my feet and gazed at the shiny pink, gray, and white marble structure. In spite of the heat, it was hard to take my eyes off the laced stonework and soaring spires of the city's great cathedral.

A street vendor interrupted me, asking in broken English if I wanted to buy a selfie stick.

I responded in Portuguese.

He left me alone.

The boys came rumbling across the piazza with their posse in tow. I was thrilled at the chance to meet the enthusiastic young Italians who had taken it upon themselves to promote the boys' music throughout their city. Before saying good-bye to their fans, Jordan and Tyler confirmed their plan to meet up with them later that evening. When the team arrived, it was time to search for the final resting place of Ambrose, the great philosopher, orator, and pastor whose teaching led to the conversion of our man of the hour, Saint Augustine.

The Basilica di Sant'Ambrogio was interesting for more reasons than just being the place that sparked Augustine's conversion. For starters, it was built over the burial site of some of the earliest Christian martyrs. In the lowest room of the church, the remains of those martyrs, along with the church's famous pastor himself, are on display. Back in the nave of the basilica, placards guide the curious through the life of Ambrose, his interactions with Augustine, and the history that followed.

THE SEARCH FOR MEANING

Augustine was born in AD 354 in North Africa to a pagan Roman official and a Christian mother named Monica. Monica was a devout woman who prayed faithfully for her husband and son. During Augustine's adolescence, she admonished him to avoid sex outside of marriage and other forms of sexual immorality. The young man interpreted this as "womanish"[1] advice and set about ignoring it.

At seventeen years of age, Augustine moved to Carthage, Italy, where "outrageous loves," as he described them, wooed his adolescent desires. He wasn't yet in love but was "in love with love."[2] In this deep emotional and spiritual hunger, he tenaciously sought to satisfy his cravings through a "cauldron of illicit loves."[3] His drunken indulgence of the sensual lifestyle left him with broken relationships and created in him jealousies, anger, and eventually regret and a deep emptiness.

In the midst of his carnal quests, Augustine set about studying the discipline of rhetoric, the art of elegant and convincing communication. While studying in Carthage, he encountered a book by Cicero titled *Hortensius.* This book dramatically altered the course of Augustine's life. He wrote that it "changed my emotional direction" and that "all vain ambition became vile to me all of a sudden."[4] This evoked in Augustine a new passion for the study of philosophy, which, according to Cicero, could be defined as the "love of wisdom."

To clarify, this wasn't a conversion to a new faith but rather a shifting of priorities. Augustine was famous for praying during this time, "God, give me chastity ... but not yet."

"He had a new ideal, not a new way of life."[5]

In time he formed a deep connection with Manichaeism, a form of religious dualism (two supreme powers that equally oppose one another) that claimed one must have special knowledge and learn a complex mythology to know God. This appealed to Augustine's intellect and high regard for reason. Although he would eventually abandon this religious doctrine, the experience provoked in him questions that would influence his understanding of faith for the rest of his life.

At twenty years of age, having completed his studies, Augustine returned home and became a teacher. However, after the death of a friend, he found it unbearable to remain and moved back to Carthage, where he opened a school of rhetoric. This venture didn't last long, however. Frustrated with his unruly students, he moved again, this time to Rome, where he plied his trade and sought to dispense his knowledge in this center of world influence. Unfortunately, the Italian students failed to remunerate him for his services. Frustrated again, at age thirty, Augustine accepted an invitation to become a professor of rhetoric in Milan. His mother went with him, still praying and hoping that her son would convert to Christianity.

Her prayers were answered.

Dissatisfied with his Manichaeistic beliefs and exasperated by the lack of sustained pleasure and fulfillment life had thus far afforded him, Augustine embarked on a quest to understand the origins of his needs, desires, and compulsions. It was in Milan where Augustine became fascinated with the teachings of Ambrose. Through these teachings and his mother's prayers, the truths of Jesus Christ finally met the longing in his soul.

ANTICIPATION

Longing. I know this sensation well—an intense conflagration of love and loneliness.

Well-known psychologist Gerald May identifies *longing* as a "passionate yearning for ... something" and writes, "I called it my longing for God, and of course that's what all our deepest longings really are, but I could just as well have said it was a longing for love, for union, for fully being in life, for being vitally connected with everything."[6]

As I write, autumn is falling into winter, and like a lava flow beneath the surface of our days, the anticipation for Christmas warms our nights. For many reasons Christmas is our family's favorite holiday. But do you know what perhaps is even more enjoyable than Christmas?

Anticipating Christmas.

Anticipation is a strange cocktail of excitement, sadness, and joy.

Longing is real. Undeniable. I want something. I yearn for something. Most of the time I'm not even sure what that something is. Although the older I get, the more I'm convinced it's "a sense of interior exuberance"[7] that manifests itself in connection with the Creator and His creation.

But anticipation is a bit different from longing. The chasm between longing and anticipation seems to be traversed only by faith. Without belief in someone or something, longing has the power to dominate our thoughts and subjugate our behavior. Anticipation is longing fused with hope.

With anticipation, I'm aware there is something I'm not yet experiencing. *Yet* being the operative word. While I'm sad in my waiting, I'm hopeful in that something's arrival. I time-travel ahead and can already taste the joy I'm convinced will follow.

I think this is one reason the church during Advent chooses the word *anticipation* as one of four themes. The word *advent* means coming or arrival and is the season of preparation leading up to Christmas Day, the celebration of the incarnation of Christ. Many churches symbolically light four candles, one on each of the four Sundays before Christmas. The four candles represent varying themes in varying faith traditions. Our church recently celebrated these four Advent themes: longing, anticipation, preparation, and expectation.

Anticipation pulls us into future celebration.

After filming our segment in front of Ambrose's church, I watched Jordan and Tyler perform a street show at the Palazzo Lombardia. Surrounding the plaza were beautifully constructed modern buildings whose curved glass and sinuous lines stirred in me a sense of cheerful yet peaceful motion. Set up in front of the UniCredit Tower, one of the tallest buildings in Italy, the boys played a small set of covers and originals, collecting curious spectators and making memories with their fans.

On the subway back to our hotel, we caught up on their experiences of the day. The boys shared that some of their conversations coursed deep. Several of the girls they talked with spoke of the weight of internal loneliness and longing but had no concept of a personal God in nature. If anything, they viewed Him as more of a historical figure. My sons' new Italian friends described in detail the brokenness of relationships that surrounded them, and how their wish for meaningful love seemed unattainable.

A HOLY LONGING

Augustine spent three decades seeking love, pleasure, and the meaning of life. He sought to satiate his longings with unbridled sexual indulgence. He pursued philosophy and logic in an attempt to quell the haunting whispers of his soul. He adopted different belief systems to try to quench his irrepressible thirst for something more.

At most, these diversions offered only temporary relief. Why?

Why do we have unmet longings woven into our existence?

Why do we ache when true desires, expectations, and needs go unfulfilled?

Perhaps it's because we're designed to be *fulfilled*.

> *[God] has also set eternity in the human heart; yet no one*
> *can fathom what God has done from beginning to end.*[8]
> King Solomon

A longing is buried deep inside each of us for wrongs to be made right, for someone with the ability and power to change defeat to victory. Sometimes this yearning is so strong we can't bear it anymore, and for most of us, we learn to numb. Shut down. Close off.

But we're never fully successful, are we?

This longing for things to be made right is an echo from eternity. It's a huge billboard sign. An important reminder.

We're right to wish for more.

We're right to search for answers to our questions.

We're right to expect something beyond death.

We're right to scream at its absence here on earth.

We're to weep over its delay.

It's not only okay to have a longing for justice, pleasure, and fulfillment; it would be a tragedy to live without it.

If I find in myself a desire which no experience in this world can satisfy, the most probable explanation is that I was made for another world.[9]
C. S. Lewis

With every aching heartbeat, we should be reminded that this feeling of wrongness and extreme longing for rightness points us toward something. Someone.

Rightness has a name.

Jesus.

Jesus has invited us into the city of God, a Kingdom like no other. One day there will be no more weeping, no more death, no more darkness, no more emptiness, no more fear, and no more loneliness. Our yearning will end. Rightness will rule.

Our longing has a deadline.

FINDING FULFILLMENT

In Milan, Augustine was engrossed in the insight and skill of the city's most famous orator, Ambrose. In him Augustine saw what it looked like to be a Christian as well as an intellectual.

Once a reluctant bishop, Ambrose became highly regarded and exceedingly influential in Milan. Augustine was eager to hear the celebrated speaker. Their first meeting was likely after a Sunday service and was quite casual, but Augustine felt an instant connection with this great man. In time Ambrose's explanations of Scripture as allegory and metaphor made a profound impact on Augustine. His interest in the Holy Scriptures was piqued, and his heart began to soften.

Ambrose taught that for one to understand the Scriptures, one must obtain the key. The key to unlocking understanding was faith in Christ and illumination from the Spirit.

The letter kills, but the Spirit gives life.[10]
Paul the apostle

On an autumn day in AD 386, thirty-two-year-old Augustine, agitated in soul and feeling the violence of shame, ran outside his rented home and collapsed in tears under a fig tree. The stories of others finding faith and freedom in God were creating in Augustine a realization of his own self-hatred. For the first time in his life he addressed God. "How long, Lord? Will you be angry with me forever?" His despondency was interrupted when he heard a child's voice say, "Take it and read, take it and read."[11] Augustine got up and walked back inside toward his gaming table, where he had left a book that held a collection of the apostle Paul's letters. He found Paul's message to the Romans, and the result has been called "one of the most dramatic conversions to Christ ever recorded."[12]

Augustine was baptized and began to devote his time to studying Scripture. He became particularly fond of the Psalms and quoted them often. Leaving his teaching position in Milan, Augustine decided to return to North Africa with his mother, where some believe he had in mind that he would live at a monastic retreat, spending his days thinking and writing. While he and his mother were on a stopover in a port town, however, she became ill and died nine days later. Augustine wrote of the devastating loss, "My soul was wounded, and that life rent asunder as it were, which, of hers and mine together, had been made but one."[13]

Augustine's firm belief that his mother's soul had gone on to heaven softened the blow, however. He found great comfort in this.

Continuing his travels, he visited a friend in the port town of Hippo (modern day Algeria), where local church leaders pressed him into becoming a priest and taking on a congregation. Augustine was reluctant at first, but he eventually relented.

And he never moved again.

After the local bishop's death, Augustine took his place and served this church faithfully until his death at age seventy-six.

It was in relationship with others, in the dirt of people's lives, that he wrote most of his works, including *Confessions* and *The City of God*, which would make him "the most influential theologian in the entire Latin-speaking church since New Testament times."[14]

GOD'S ORIGINAL DESIGN

With tremendous insight and vulnerability, Augustine shared his spiritual pilgrimage in his autobiography, *Confessions*. He wrote at length about the will of humankind and the initiative of God. "Man, when he was created, received great powers of free will, but lost them by sinning." He believed that "man, using free will badly, has lost both himself and his will."[15] He also spoke boldly of the destructive nature of pride: "What is pride but the craving for undue exaltation. And this is undue exaltation, when the soul abandons Him to whom it ought to cleave as its end."[16]

Pride is always at the root of our sin. Think about it.

Where does your drive for control come from?

What are you afraid of?

Do you believe, ultimately, that the only person you can trust to take care of you is you?

What do you not believe about God?

These questions confront us with our willingness or unwillingness to trust. The fall of humanity marred God's beautiful creation with a propensity toward self-reliance. Our sin compels us to function as supreme rulers, and when we sin, we distance ourselves from God's original design. We fail to meet the glorious goal that God had for who we would become as human creatures: "The technical term for that is 'sin,' whose primary meaning is not '*breaking the rules*' but '*missing the mark*,' failing to hit the target of complete, genuine, glorious humanness."[17]

If sin is about breaking the rules, then we're forever in reactionary mode. Why? Because it's impossible for us to consistently keep the rules. The pressure to perform will eventually give way to hopelessness, despair, or internal self-loathing.

And if sin is about obeying rules, then obey we must, dutifully, with little attention to the heart. We must curtail, repress, and restrain our behaviors. And in many ways this characterizes our initial spiritual journeys. Most of us try to find God through our own righteousness. We remove the tension of trusting Him, but fabricating formulas, we trust those instead.

Augustine, after his conversion, got rid of his mistress and her son. In his desire to eliminate his craving for sexual satisfaction, he removed from his life the object of his affection and, swinging the proverbial pendulum in the opposite direction, chose chastity. I'm not saying this was right or wrong for Augustine, but what if Augustine had instead married this woman and loved and nurtured their son in the ways of God?

Maybe the hardest relationships in our lives are the ones in which God is most present. Sometimes "God comes to us disguised as our life."[18]

I've learned something about love. It's costly.

Jesus limited access to His own power to bear the consequences of our sin. By deferring this right, He allowed our race to mock and embarrass Him and then slaughter Him along a public road.

Love doesn't exist without sacrifice.

"Love without truth is sentimentality; it supports and affirms us but keeps us in denial about our flaws. Truth without love is harshness; it gives us information but in such a way that we cannot really hear it. God's saving love in Christ, however, is marked by both radical truthfulness about who we are and yet also radical, unconditional commitment to us."[19]

"The gospel is this: We are more sinful and flawed in ourselves than we ever dared believe, yet at the very same time we are more loved and accepted in Jesus Christ than we ever dared hope."[20]

The truth that you're flawed is meant not to make you feel ashamed but to make you feel hopeful. Some of you may cringe at that, saying to yourselves, "I already think I'm a depraved sinner. How much worse can it get?" Sin becomes an awareness and reminder that something isn't right. We have a tragic impairment. But the conviction of God's Spirit produces repentance followed by hope.

Victimization, on the other hand, breeds shame. Many of us spend a lifetime looking for a solution to our lonely ache. And oh how we try so many different ways to make it go away.

Some of us buy into the lie that marriage or some other significant relationship will solve the tragic impairment in our lives. *My loneliness will go away. I will finally feel secure about myself. My needs will now be met.* The problem is, we have drifted away from what George MacDonald referred to as "the holy Present." God is making Himself known to us every moment. But rather than listen for His voice, we look past Him, our eyes blinded to the Kingdom around us, and fall into step with this earthly kingdom and whatever idols are presently available to meet our needs.

> *It is our experiences that transform us if we are willing to experience our experiences all the way through.*[21]
> Richard Rohr

Augustine expounded on this in his literary masterpiece *The City of God*. In this book he contrasted two cities, or kingdoms, that are each built on the premise of love: "The city of God is built on the love of God. The earthly city is built on the love of self.... In the end only the city of God will remain.... [The] kingdoms and nations, all built on love of self, ... are no more than passing expressions of the earthly city."[22]

In his book, Augustine explained the yearning within by highlighting the teachings of Jesus, who throughout His earth walk would tell anyone who would listen that the Kingdom of God was at hand. At one point when Jesus described this alternate reality, He said, "The King will say to those on his right, 'Come, you who are blessed by my Father; take your inheritance, the kingdom prepared for you since the creation of the world.'"[23]

This Kingdom has a King. His name is Jesus. He offers His followers an inheritance. And while we have access to a portion of this inheritance in our lifetimes, it seems we don't receive it in full until the next life. The transition that leads to being fully absorbed into this Kingdom reality is death. In Augustine's city of self-love, "man's natural thought of death is that of a dreary ending in decay and dissolution. And from his standpoint he is right: death as the punishment of sin is an ending. But far other is God's thought in the redemption of the world. He takes the very thing that came in with the curse and makes it the path of glory. Death becomes a beginning instead of an ending, for it becomes the means of liberating a fresh life."[24]

Jesus taught about the consummation of the soul's great longing: "Did I not tell you that if you believe, you will see the glory of God?"[25]

We each have a desire to be included in something magnificent. When we know God, we do more than long for it. We anticipate it. In the anticipation, we believe.

And when we believe, just like Augustine, we're immersed in glory.

Chapter 8

THE WAY OF
HUMILITY

Saint Francis of Assisi, AD 1181–1226, Assisi, Italy

Nothing else but you, oh Lord.
"I Surrender," All Sons & Daughters

The fervent sun beat down on our team as we trekked up a sprawling hill that adorned the Italian countryside. Lugging extra pounds of gear made for a strenuous and sweaty climb, but undeterred we plodded along. Finally reaching Basilica di San Francesco d'Assisi, we were quickly rewarded with a sweeping vista of mountainside vineyards and sunflower fields glimmering in the morning light. Turning toward the great basilica that housed the final remains of its namesake, we made our way across the piazza.

Several of us had already been wondering if this small village of Assisi might be the climax of our venture. The story of Saint Francis had enamored Leslie, in particular, for some time, and my enthusiasm was cresting, since I had been reading through a biography on his life.

Assisi did not disappoint.

Before we entered the part of the basilica called the Upper Church, a young man in a gray tunic and baseball cap stopped us. Speaking perfect English, he identified himself as Friar Andrew, a monk belonging to the Franciscan Order. In moments we struck up a friendly conversation.

Team members shared the purpose of our journey and offered up stories from our adventure. Friar Andrew, a man who looked to be in his late twenties, shared his intriguing story in return. The child of Protestant missionaries in Turkey, he became intrigued by Saint Francis while studying in Indiana at the University of Notre Dame. Deeply struck by the man's legacy, Friar Andrew moved to Italy to give himself to the order. He explained that while he had sacrificed much for this life calling, he had also experienced great joy.

Friar Andrew spends most of his days praying for people as they make their pilgrimage to Assisi, the final resting place of Saint Francis. We asked if we could pray with him. Regarding us with kind eyes and a big smile, he replied, "Yes, I would love that." After concluding our prayer, I noticed our new friend had tears in his eyes. In a soft voice he said, "I spend so much time praying for strangers, I didn't realize how meaningful it would be to have strangers pray for me."

We knew in our hearts that we were strangers no longer, and we made plans to meet up later that afternoon.

THE YOUNG REBEL

Saint Francis influenced church history in far-reaching and even unimaginable ways. I'm sure you've driven through your town at Christmastime and seen a nativity scene displayed on a front lawn or two. Perhaps you've even set one up yourself. If so, Saint Francis has touched your life.

Desiring to celebrate the true meaning of Christmas, during midnight Mass in 1223, Francis set up a manger scene complete with hay and live animals to recreate and honor the birth of Christ. The experience was so moving that this dramatic presentation would eventually become a worldwide tradition.

Francis became widely known for his love and appreciation of nature and animals. Gerald May wrote, "What none of us seems to want, what we all resist, is to admit that we are inevitably, intimately, and irrevocably part of Nature rather than apart from it."[1] We were created from the earth and will be forever connected to it. Francis valued God's creation in such a way that he treated it with dignity and great worth.

Francis was more than just devoted to God's creation, however. By modeling self-restraint and self-sacrifice, he set the trajectory for a new kind of Catholic in his day. At a time of moral and political upheaval in the church, Francis exemplified the way of humility. To this day the

Franciscan Order, followers of God who adhere to the saint's teaching, continues to flourish and influence the world. To understand why Francis valued what he did and how he knew God the way he did, let's explore his story.

*The coming of St. Francis was like the birth of a child in a
dark house, lifting its doom; a child that grows up unconscious
of the tragedy and triumphs over it by his innocence.*[2]

G. K. Chesterton

Named Giovanni di Pietro di Bernardone at birth and later nicknamed Francesco, Francis was born in the late twelfth century in the small Italian town of Assisi. His father Pietro, a seller of cloths and dyes, was a very successful merchant. Though the class system was still in place, cultural shifts were having an influence on it, and consequently, the social structure was slowly beginning to change. While Francis's family wasn't part of the nobility, his father's business was so prosperous that before long they gained influence among the elite. Scaling the social ladder gave their family a certain prestige; however, it's worth noting that Pietro didn't become successful accidentally. He was shrewd and ruthless in his dealings and became used to getting his own way.

Francis's mother, according to tradition, was a beautiful woman who loved history and literature. She seems to be the one who opened a portal for her son into a world of imagination. From the time he was a child, it is said that she would spin tales of the magnificent conquests of great knights. Like most boys of that era, Francis probably loved the story of Charlemagne. As a young man, Francis dreamed about becoming someone of great significance, someone famous, perhaps even a knight that people would tell stories about to their children.

To his father's great disappointment, Francis made it pretty clear as a teenager that he had no interest in following in his dad's footsteps. The young man seemed to always be trying to pull away from his father and his demanding expectations. Francis was rebellious and impertinent. As rebels often do, he had great charisma and striking leadership qualities. Before long he gathered a posse of his friends, and according to biographer Robert West, they became known as the "Sons of Babylon."[3] Let's just say this wasn't the crowd your mother would want you to run with. The gang was made up of a bunch of hellions. They polluted the town with their raucous behavior and drunkenness, wreaking havoc and disturbing the peace.

Pietro was not pleased. He expected his son to be industrious and not waste his time on frivolous pursuits. He didn't refrain from giving Francis money, however, and Francis didn't refrain from spending it. Still nursing the childhood dream of becoming a knight, the young man hired an instructor who trained him in the art of warfare.

Most young men with an innate zeal to prove themselves dream about some type of physical competition in which they come out on top. John Eldredge writes that deep "in the heart of every man is a desperate desire for a battle to fight, an adventure to live, and a beauty to rescue."[4] I can relate to this. Strategy and combat have always fascinated me, and had I not entered adolescence during the Cold War, I might have considered enlisting in the military.

In my thirties I watched the movie *Saving Private Ryan* with my friend Lee. Any illusions about the glamour or purpose of war were stripped away after watching that film. Steven Spielberg was so proficient in portraying the humanity of the soldiers that for me it was difficult to look at combat in an impersonal way anymore. The violence that had previously intrigued me now left me feeling sad and reticent.

Francis would have to come to grips with his own desires for conquest and glory.

TO BECOME A KNIGHT

Francis's dreams of going to battle came true in his twenties. Hostility was brewing between the village of Assisi and their sworn enemy Perugia. Francis joined with the nobles and others from surrounding areas to fight in the Battle of Collestrada.

This was the day Francis had dreamed about. We can only imagine how it unfolded ...

He rose early and, outfitted with a suit of armor awash with splendid colors, mounted his steed and rode into the brisk, foggy Italian morning. Excitement hung in the air as a crowd gathered in the town square to wish their warriors success. Mothers wiped back tears, fearful for their grown boys, while fathers suppressed their fears with pride. Standing with their chests puffed out, they nodded to their sons, a sign of approval. Suddenly a cheer rang out through the masses. Francis, enthralled by the dramatic scene, spun his horse in a tight circle, waved to the crowd, and then galloped off with his armored comrades into the morning mist. Finally Francis was a knight.

History reveals that the town suffered a disastrous loss. Though Assisian forces set out advantageously, taking the high ground, they were quickly outmaneuvered. Francis witnessed many of his friends dying on the battlefield.

Apparently, because of Francis's splendid suit of armor, the enemy assumed he was a man worth something. So instead of killing him, the Perugians captured and imprisoned him with other knights and nobles. These weary and devastated men were locked in a guarded dungeon, where they awaited the terms of ransom.

During Francis's imprisonment, something began to change in him. The life he had known as a pampered, rich, spoiled brat transformed overnight to that of a defeated soldier and prisoner living in a damp, cold dungeon, his new home for almost a year. The time wasn't wasted, however. Francis learned from the men around him. With rapt attention, he listened to their stories and in captivity forged numerous relationships that would last a lifetime.

Eventually his father paid the ransom for his son's freedom. After arriving home and reconnecting with old friends, Francis resumed the party life for a while. But things were different this time around. He had left captivity gravely ill. Most historians believe that while in prison, he had contracted malaria, which severely and permanently compromised his immune system. But Francis suffered from more than a physical malady; a spiritual tension began to rise in his soul. Though he wasn't actively serving others, his experience in the dungeon opened his eyes to the pain in the world and the plight of the impoverished.

Still, a part of him was consumed by a personal quest for glory. And within a year, he had another shot.

The fourth crusade called for soldiers, and once again, with about eight other men from Assisi, Francis galloped off to pursue the romance of battle. Not farther than a day's ride from town, he became ill and fell behind. Alone on his trotting horse, he was surprised to hear a voice.

"Who can do more good for you, the lord or the servant?"

A bit delirious and unsure where the voice was coming from, Francis answered, "The lord, of course!" He didn't have God in mind, however, but a powerful man, such as a landowner or noble.

A follow-up question resonated in the quiet countryside: "Then why are you abandoning the lord for the servant?"[5]

As Francis rode along contemplating these words, his thinking shifted. He finally realized that this was the voice of God and that "the lord" this voice spoke of was the Son of God. Francis immediately turned his horse around and headed back to Assisi. In the face of potential embarrassment, he rode through the familiar streets and retired to his home. Removing his beloved suit of armor, Francis began wrestling with his experience on the road and its deeper meaning.

Six months later, news arrived in town. The region's entire army had been ambushed and massacred. Had Francis remained with his comrades, he would have been killed. Lost in a quandary over life's purpose and preoccupied with the needs of the poor, Francis found that his exploits with friends no longer held pleasure. He determined that unlike his tendencies in the past, he would never again refuse a man who asked something of him, whether time or possessions.

Francis became progressively attuned to the needs of those around him. Through this growing empathy and compassion, he was getting to know the heart of God. He was accepting his inadequacy to perform perfectly and recognizing that salvation was found in Christ alone.

There is so much from Francis's life to draw inspiration from. This season of his life is deeply revealing and, I believe, apropos for the church in our current Western culture. We haven't been called to fix people and teach them to cope. God has called us to love them in their brokenness and invite and nudge them toward the great Redeemer. By serving those in great need, Francis learned to have a heart of compassion. When we're involved in the grit of people's brokenness, we quickly learn that their physical and emotional conditions don't change overnight. For most of us, even our spiritual awakening and maturation require time.

Francis was experiencing conversion, a process peppered with experiences that would bring him closer and closer to God. His encounter with a leper solidified his yearning to know the Creator. At that time, people suffering from leprosy, the bacterial disease that deteriorates the flesh and often causes a loss of limbs, were regarded as social outcasts and were ordered to remain on the fringes of society. Subjected to life in isolated communities, when they emerged, lepers were forced to shake rattles to warn others of their approach. These ailing, disfigured pariahs had repulsed and offended Francis all his life. But this day, walking along the road, when Francis heard the rattling sound and saw a leper walk toward him, he felt a lump rise in his throat. Yet he was compelled not to run the other way or ignore the man but to go to him.

I imagine he swallowed hard and suppressed his nausea before approaching the leper, who was probably shaking his rattle like a madman at that point. When Francis got close enough to the maimed fellow, he grabbed the man's hands and kissed them. Then he placed in those mangled hands what few coins he had. The leper limped away astounded, shaking his head in disbelief as a cloud of dust trailed behind. What had just happened was incomprehensible. *Someone came close. Someone touched me.*

> *When nothing is foreign to us nobody will be foreign to*
> *us—and our words will begin to heal others.*[6]
>
> Ronald Rolheiser

In that moment, when Francis walked headlong into such an aversion, into a place where he felt fear and disgust, he was transformed. The Spirit of God poured through him with a renewed and profound love.

"REBUILD MY CHURCH"

Armed with a rising passion to serve God, Francis would take long walks, praying and seeking the true Father of all humankind. On one such walk through the woods, he came upon a little, dilapidated church named San Damiano. He heard a voice that said, "Go in and pray." So he did. As Francis prayed before an old crucifix that dangled above the altar, "the painted form of the crucified Christ on the crucifix suddenly moved its lips." And then he heard, "Francis, don't you see that my house is being destroyed? Go and repair my house, which, as you see, is falling completely into ruin."[7]

Though the experience shook him and moved him to act, Francis wasn't really sure what to do. So he found the local priest who was responsible for the woodland and said, "Here, I've sold my horse and everything that I have, and I want to give the money to you. I'm supposed to help rebuild the church. Can I stay with you?"[8]

At first the priest didn't believe him. Between Francis's unruly character and the unbecoming reputation of his quick-tempered father, the priest was hesitant to take the young man seriously. Francis tried to convince him otherwise, promising that if the priest let him stay, he would prove his dedication. The priest accepted the offer but refused the money. Seeing his mission as obeying God's voice and rebuilding that run-down church, Francis put the money on the windowsill anyway.

Every day he would spend time in prayer, toil away at the building, eat, and sleep. Then he'd get up the next day and do it all over again.

Hearing the stories of his son's crazy behavior, agitated that Francis had abandoned the family business, and angered that his son had given his money to a church, Pietro hunted Francis down.

Learning of his father's impending arrival, Francis abandoned his work, climbed into a deep pit that he had found underneath the church, and hid there. For an entire month, the man lived in that hole, avoiding his father and praying that God would give him wisdom to know what to do. A close friend brought him food each day, but other than that occasional interaction, Francis remained in isolation, lost in his confusion regarding God's desire for his life and in his fear of his earthly father's demands.

After a month, Francis finally emerged from his hole in the earth.

As I reflect on his story, it seems that in many ways this emergence represented Francis's rebirth. While his suffering was far from over, something, or Someone, had clearly changed him. Brother Leo, a man who would become Francis's most trusted companion and secretary, wrote that God's Spirit filled Francis "with an inexpressible happiness and enlightened him with a marvelous light."[9] Emaciated, yet full of joy, Francis stumbled back to Assisi demonstrably praising God on his way.

> *The true story of every person in this world is not the*
> *story you see, the external story. The true story of each*
> *person is the journey of his or her heart.*[10]
>
> John Eldredge

To the townsfolk, Francis looked like a lunatic. They mocked and scorned the man as he made his way through the village. When his father received word that his son had appeared and was embarrassing the family with his nonsensical behavior, the enraged man rushed from his shop, found his son, dragged him back to his house, and locked him in a room.

Pietro tried to talk Francis out of whatever religious or self-sacrificial life he was trying to live, but his words fell on deaf ears. Francis repeatedly told his father that he wasn't going to change but was committed to living a life of poverty. This didn't go over well. Feeling very much betrayed, Pietro spent hours arguing with his son, to no avail. Distressed at the exercise in futility, he'd then beat Francis and leave him chained in the room. Francis, however, was finding purpose in life. In spite of his father's abuse, and perhaps because of it, he was determined more than ever to live differently.

Francis's mother often stood between father and son. Once she understood the depth of her son's conviction, she helped Francis escape. When Pietro discovered what she had done, he was so angry that he beat her. Then he found his son and, still raging, threatened that if Francis didn't return home at once, he would disown the young man. For Francis, at least for now, this possibility was a relief.

THE FATHER WOUND

It's obvious in Francis's story that the wounds from his father ran deep. Nursing a grudge, Pietro didn't keep quiet long. Eventually he reneged on his promise and pursued Francis with a passion, demanding he pay back all the money he had given to his earlier church project, since, technically, it was his father's money. Francis didn't respond, so his father took him to court. When the young man didn't show up on the appointed day, the powers that be dismissed the matter, saying it was too petty for their involvement. Without legal recourse Pietro approached the town's church leaders and told the bishop that he wanted to formally renounce his son and wanted back every dime that Francis had given the church. The bishop agreed to hold a trial and summoned Francis and the priest from San Damiano.

Sometime before the trial, which was scheduled for early March 1207, the bishop, knowing that Francis had sold some of his father's cloth in order to get money to help rebuild a church, pulled the young man aside and encouraged him to return his father's money. Consequently, just before the official event began, Francis walked up to his father and with hands outstretched gave him back every dime.

But he didn't stop there.

On this freezing winter day, Francis also removed all his clothes and, completely naked, handed the rumpled and worn garments to his father: "From now on I can freely say 'Our Father who art in heaven,' not father Pietro di Bernardone, to whom, behold, I give up, not only the money, but all my clothes too."[11]

> *The kingdom of heaven is like treasure hidden in a field. When a*
> *man found it, he hid it again, and then in his joy went and sold*
> *all he had and bought that field. Again, the kingdom of heaven is*

like a merchant looking for fine pearls. When he found one of great
value, he went away and sold everything he had and bought it.[12]

Jesus

Observing the scene from a few feet away, the bishop was touched by this display of strength and nonviolent, direct action. Francis had turned the tables. Rather than let his father shame him, Francis spoke directly to the deeper issue at hand. He gave up literally everything, stripping his dad of authority and control.

There was no triumph for the abusive father. As a matter of fact, if anything, the people took pity on Francis and looked at Pietro as a man without compassion. As Francis stood exposed in body and soul, the bishop took off his mantle and put it around the young man, which, while physically clothing his nakedness, also symbolized a transfer of dignity and respect. That bishop and, in time, other men would become mentoring father figures in Francis's life.

Biographer Robert West indicates that immediately after Francis accepted the tunic from the bishop, in a state of euphoria he ran out of the great hall of the church and into the frigid outdoors. Ecstatic, he danced his way through the soft snow that blanketed the ground while singing psalms and songs. He literally danced his way twenty miles to another city.

Francis was finally free.

The system of domination that so many adhered to, the abuse, the "power-over" style of control, and the expectations of his abuser no longer had power over him. He had faced his demons and removed himself from the shackles of his parents' wealth: "He not only didn't have anything, he was free of the desire to have anything."[13]

Sure, Francis was poor. But he was free.

This reminds me of the many conversations I've had with young men and women who have felt the weight of their parents' expectations. Some have been abused or abandoned. Others have moms or dads who are passive-aggressive or unpredictable.

Breaking free from the enmeshment of a codependent parent, friend, or partner might be one of life's hardest quests and greatest points of pain, but until we do this, we'll forever be shackled to the whims of another. Anthony de Mello describes this poignantly: "For when you cling, what you offer the other is not love but a chain by which both you and your beloved are bound. Love can only exist in freedom. The true lover seeks the good of his beloved which requires especially the liberation of the beloved from the lover.... Contrary to popular beliefs, the cure for lovelessness and loneliness is not company but contact with Reality."[14]

Francis found freedom in Reality. His name is Jesus.

FOLLOWING JESUS

The process of conversion happened in Francis's heart over the course of time. Through his experience in the dungeon, through hearing the voice on the road, through his attraction to serving the poor, through his time rebuilding the church, through standing up to his father, Francis was being transformed. He was finding Jesus and renouncing himself.

Though Francis was discovering exuberant happiness, as life teaches us all, happiness isn't sustainable.

Francis experienced this certitude in its fullest extent. The day he danced for twenty miles barefoot in the snow to another city, he was left with nowhere to go. Prepared to embrace a life of extreme poverty, he assumed the local monastery would be a welcoming place. Hungry and freezing, Francis knocked on the front door. He received only alms and was treated rudely. Francis's joy was met with a proverbial bucket of cold water. Or, in this case, an evening spent in a snowbank.

Isn't this like us?

We find ourselves on a mountaintop. Experiencing intimacy with God. Closeness with the Divine.

Then we get sucker punched.

Betrayal, shame, addiction, brokenness, distraction, failure, disappointment—something knocks us down. We tumble from the peak and lie in a heap in the valley. Sprawled on our backs, we stare at the sky, somehow forgetting the moments of euphoria we just experienced, and we wonder with tears in our eyes if we'll ever get back to that wonderful place again.

The human condition. Fickle and fleeting.

The goodness of God. Patient and persevering.

It would be nice to note that in Francis's story, his father came around and eventually supported his son. He didn't.

Nonetheless, Francis pushed through. His love for his heavenly Father became all-consuming.

Assisi became the nerve center of his ministry. The playboy who had previously spent his nights partying in the city streets, now, having given everything away, walked them with compassion. He helped restore other church buildings, and one in particular, known as Porziuncola, the little chapel of Saint Mary of the Angels, which the abbot of Saint Benedict of Monte Subasio donated, became the home for his ministry. Francis spent the rest of his life ministering to the poor, the broken, and his fellow Franciscans.

FRIARS AND FRISBEES

As a father of four, when I think about the rejection Francis experienced from his dad, my heart hurts. I sometimes wonder what it will be like when my children become adults and have the space and discernment to consider the ways I have failed them. I don't like this feeling, but I know

THE WAY OF HUMILITY

it's a truth I cannot avoid. As much as I long to love my children well, I will fail. But observing the pain in Francis's life, I find hope. Somehow, in spite of inadequate parenting, our children will search for God.

In the afternoon after arriving in Assisi, our team reconnected with Friar Andrew. We took a break from the heat in a small café and then resumed exploring the place where Francis had dedicated so much of his life. I watched as my sons ambled up to Andrew and, one on each side, pelted him with questions about celibacy and poverty. They were captivated by his life of self-denial and devotion. Later that day, Jordan walked up to me and, pointing in the direction of Andrew, said, "He was one of the highlights of this trip. Dad, Andrew has such a love for God. I want that kind of passion. Oh, and you're not going to believe this. The man plays Frisbee!"

"What?"

"He plays Frisbee for the Turkish national team."

"Andrew, the Franciscan friar who studied in Indiana and lives in Italy, plays Frisbee for the Turkish national team?"

"Yeah, totally," Jordan responded, his eyes wide with excitement. "And he taught Pope Francis how to play! Well, not the entire sport, but he was carrying his Frisbee when he met the pope, and the pope asked him what it was for."

"What did Friar Andrew say?"

"You toss it back and forth to share joy," Jordan said with a smile.

Best definition of *Frisbee* I've ever heard.

LEAD WITH LOVE

Saint Francis had an unbending commitment to what he referred to as "Lady Poverty." Poverty wasn't the end goal but rather a pathway toward maintaining an intimate relationship with Jesus Christ. In Francis's story, the combination of excess wealth and pressure from his father had provoked his deepest pain and formed his greatest obstacles to peace and fulfillment. In his desire to be deeply known by God and in his determination to avoid the manipulative power of money, Saint Francis sought a life of deprivation.

He wasn't alone. Over time others joined his mission. Men across the social classes were drawn to the life Saint Francis had chosen, inspired by the way he lived it. With men and eventually women sharing in his dream, Francis began to realize that the calling he heard from God in the moving lips of the crucifix had a much deeper meaning than just fixing up an old building. Saint Francis was involved in a movement that, in its extreme expression, was countering the greed of the day. Those around Francis agreed it would be a good idea to begin forming guidelines and structure to better explain and protect the noble cause they were giving themselves to.

One day Francis, along with twelve close companions, traveled to the Vatican to see Pope Innocent III, one of the most influential popes ever to rule. They hoped he would formalize their cadre of followers as an "order."

There, in the midst of Roman Catholic opulence, these twelve men, with Francis as their spokesperson, pleaded their case. Initially the pope laughed off Francis. He spoke sarcastically to him (probably based on the way he was dressed), telling him in essence, "Why don't you go roll with the pigs and see if you can talk them into formalizing your order for you?"

That evening, however, unable to get Francis out of his mind, the pope sent word for the man to return the following day. When Francis arrived, not only was he still dressed informally, but he also smelled so bad that those around him turned away or covered their noses. The pope was furious. *What kind of Christian would be this insolent?*

Francis spoke, "I have done what you ordered. I beg you now to hear my petition."[15]

Taken aback by this man's audacity and passion, Pope Innocent III couldn't help but respect the vision set before him. After a brief dialogue, the Catholic rulers acknowledged Francis, and the Franciscan Order, also known as the Order of Friars Minor, was officially birthed. Francis returned home praising God.

Having heard from other priests about the church's mismanagement of funds and abuse of power, Francis set the direction for the order early on; namely, decentralizing power. He made it clear that these monks were not to be known for criticizing others for doing it wrong; rather, they were to be known for their love and for modeling what they understood to be right.

Avoiding a professional clergy culture, the Franciscan way exemplifies equality and partnership. Each member of the body contributes his or her gifts back to the whole. Throughout their history, the Franciscans have promoted a sense of belonging within their order and beyond—in the way they love each other, in the way they resolve conflict, in the way they promote reconciliation. Grace is the glue that bonds their relationships.

The stories of Saint Francis are endless, from his brazen attempt to convert an Islamic sultan to his uncanny connection with nature to his endless devotion to prayer to his preaching to the animals. But the overarching message of his life was to lead with love. This is still reflected in the Franciscan way.

Saint Francis found the pearl of great price and gave up everything to be sure that he held on to what was most valuable. Here was a man who craved to be intimate with his creator and refused to allow anything to get in the way of that relationship.

I want to exist in passionate pursuit of Jesus. I long for that singular focus Saint Francis exemplified. But unlike this saint, I make a lot of excuses. I rationalize. The stuff of my life often trips up my judgment and obedience.

What about you?

What keeps you distracted? What gets the majority of your attention?

Does your love for money cloud your judgment? Does your acquisition of things take up your time?

What are you trying to resolve by purchasing more stuff? How much time and energy will you spend managing and protecting what you've acquired?

Do you experience the "torture of repressed expression"?[16]

What are you looking for? What is it you desire?

Do you deeply want an intimate relationship with God, or is God a thing on the side?

Take in the following words from a poem of Saint Francis, translated into English and known today as the popular hymn "All Creatures of Our God and King." Listen for the intimacy he so clearly experienced with the Creator-God. Consider what it might be like to know and be known in that same way.

All creatures of our God and King
Lift up your voice and with us sing,
Alleluia! Alleluia!

Thou burning sun with golden beam,
Thou silver moon with softer gleam!

O praise Him! O praise Him!
Alleluia! Alleluia! Alleluia!

Thou rushing wind that art so strong
Ye clouds that sail in Heaven along,
O praise Him! Alleluia!

Thou rising moon, in praise rejoice,
Ye lights of evening, find a voice!

O praise Him! O praise Him!
Alleluia! Alleluia! Alleluia!

Let all things their Creator bless,
And worship Him in humbleness,
O praise Him! Alleluia!

Praise, praise the Father, praise the Son,
And praise the Spirit, Three in One![17]

Chapter 9

LIVE THE IMPOSSIBLE

Saint Peter, Died AD 65, Israel

*Humble yourselves, therefore, under God's mighty
hand, that he may lift you up in due time.*[1]

After a beautiful day in Assisi, our team loaded the bus and headed
south. I lobbied unsuccessfully for a detour to the Amalfi coast and
settled into the two-and-a-half-hour journey to Rome. Having spent
many nights sleeping on a tour-bus bunk, I looked forward to stretch-
ing out in a hotel bed. Before bedtime, the boys and I indulged in rare
personal time. I worked out, Tyler found a corner to FaceTime his
girlfriend, and Jordan took off to explore the hotel.

About an hour later, Jordan stumbled through the doorway and, with
a Krameresque look on his face, blurted out, "You are never gonna
believe what just happened!"

"What?" I asked, eyeing him with suspicion.

"I got stuck in the elevator!"

"Huh?'

"Well, I decided to go down to the lowest level of the hotel and check out the pool. The signs seemed to indicate that everything was shut down for the night, but, you know, I wanted to see the pool. So I went and checked it out. It was cool. I had a little prayer time with God and got back on the elevator. Somewhere between the floors, it got stuck! And I couldn't do anything to fix it. I punched all the buttons, jumped up and down, and knocked on the wall—nothing helped. And my phone had no service. I started to freak thinking I was going to die in an elevator in Rome!"

"So then what happened?" I asked, my voice tinged with amusement.

"Well, I finally pried open the doors, and the next floor was right above me, about shin level. So I climbed up!"

"Dang! So how did you get back here? The stairs?"

"No. The door to the stairwell was locked, so I had to take the other elevator."

"Oh, my heavens, Jordan! Weren't you thinking the whole time that it would get stuck too?"

"Well, sure, but I just kept praying that God would keep it working. I mean, I had to get back on the horse—or the elevator—as they say."

Our team gathered again for dinner, exchanging stories and prepping for the next day. Early the next morning, Tyler, Zach, and I made our way toward Saint Peter's Basilica, the papal enclave in Rome. Standing in the immense courtyard at the center of Vatican City, we stared in amazement at the majestic basilica before us. High in the air along a columned structure ringing the courtyard were statues of the many popes who had ruled in this place.

The background cacophony was overwhelming. Echoing around us was the ceaseless chatter of tour guides relinquishing their treasures of knowledge, the noise of motorists navigating their way through the city, and the prattle of thousands of pilgrims and tourists like us, trying to find their way. This made for sensory overload, and yet somehow, standing in the middle of it all, we managed to stay present and enjoy the moment.

Because Catholics consider Saint Peter the first pope, this great basilica stands at the center of the Catholic tradition. Nearby is the famous Sistine Chapel, known throughout the world for Michelangelo's ceiling fresco of God's finger reaching out to man. Millions of tourists visit this place each year and then wait for hours to catch a glimpse of Michelangelo's great masterpiece.

Sadly we didn't have time to enter the grand basilica or the chapel and instead looked for a place outside where we might shoot our segment with Saint Peter's in the background. After a Vatican guard interrupted our scouting party and scolded us for entering a location we weren't meant to enter, we opted for a shot away from the clamor of the square. We waited for the rest of the team to arrive and then, gathering under the shade of a small tree, we began to talk about the follower of Jesus whose name has dominated church history.

THE CALL

Of the dozen apprentices who became known as Jesus' disciples, Peter quickly emerged as the alpha male. Though imprudent and impulsive, he was also a man of initiative. It didn't take long before Jesus tasked him with the responsibility of leadership.

Scripture records Peter's entrance into the Jesus epic:

> Andrew, Simon Peter's brother, was one of the two who heard what John had said and who had followed Jesus. The first thing Andrew did was to find his brother Simon and tell him, "We have found the Messiah" (that is, the Christ). And he brought him to Jesus.

> Jesus looked at him and said, "You are Simon son of John. You will be called Cephas" (which, when translated, is Peter).[2]

Sometime later, in response to Peter's display of faith, Jesus told him, "You are Peter, and on this rock I will build my church."[3]

This scripture has a great deal of controversy attached to it, as many scholars see this passage in a contrary light. Some believe Jesus was saying that Peter's faith was bestowed upon him from Jesus Himself, and thus the church was built on the personhood of Christ. Others say that the church was built on Peter's testimony. The Catholic tradition holds that Peter was set in place as the foundation of the church, which is why Catholics identify Peter as the first pope. And since Peter served the people of Rome, the Catholic Church centers its authority in this city.

While for centuries Catholics and Protestants have debated the expression of this dispensation of authority Jesus gave to Peter, what isn't in question is Peter's influence on millions of people throughout history.

Although Peter had many embarrassing moments, at other times he stood tall in his apprenticeship with Jesus. The book of Matthew records that he was the first disciple to recognize Jesus as the Christ. The book of Luke indicates he was the first of the men to see the risen Lord. After God's Spirit came to indwell His apostles, Peter was the first to preach a sermon with great power to the masses. He was also instrumental in breaking down the barriers of tension and misunderstanding between the Jewish people and the Gentiles.

In discussing Saint Peter's influence, our researcher in the group, Sarah, identified what she believed to be the reason people of faith might balk at studying the saints. She suggested that it turns many off to see how these beautiful but imperfect human beings have been objectified and idolized throughout history. Rather than acknowledge these saints and their impact on faith, many swing the pendulum in the other direction and ignore their contributions.

Leslie agreed. And she spoke for all of us when she shared that her enthusiasm in pursuing the lives of these poets and saints stemmed from examining the way their lives intersected with the life of Jesus. Though we refrain from worshipping followers of Christ, they continue to inspire us, and we're drawn to the ways God used them.

One of the ways we get to know God is by getting to know His people. We look back and remember. With enough reflection and study, the past dispenses illumination for the future. This can be a source of great comfort, because the future is characterized by the unknown. It can be daunting. Even dark.

Why is the future so obscure?

Why is it that God often doesn't let us see beyond our first few steps?

Why does it seem that what we long for is a forever away?

Jesus' followers asked the same questions, and He frequently left them in the tension of the unknown, placing His disciples in predicaments where they would have to make decisions without adequate information. There's something about the absence of control that reminds us we aren't the authors of our own stories.

INTO THE STORM

While Peter is known for many things, his water walk is perhaps most familiar because it speaks loudly to our primal hopes and fears. The story is recorded in the book of Matthew.

Jesus had been teaching an audience of thousands on the shore of the Sea of Galilee. After providing a miraculous meal for them, He sent them home for the evening. Then He ushered His disciples away too, asking them to get in a boat and head across the lake. Matthew wrote that "immediately Jesus made the disciples get into the boat and go on ahead of him to the other side, while he dismissed the crowd."[4]

I suspect the reason the text says Jesus "made" them get into the boat is that these men were fishermen. Invariably they understood weather patterns. Accustomed to life by the sea, they probably looked at the darkening sky and, feeling the wind pick up, knew that getting into the boat was risky business.

When I visited Israel, and in particular the Sea of Galilee, the locals explained that from out of nowhere and with little warning, winds channeling through the nearby mountain range can violently whip across the lake. I've visited the sea on several occasions, and one night as I was standing on the shore with my friend Ben, the wind blew with such force, it nearly knocked us over.

Despite the disciples' probable hemming and hawing, it seemed Jesus was resolute in His request. So the men obeyed and took off across the lake, leaving Jesus alone.

> After [Jesus] had dismissed them, he went up on a mountainside by himself to pray. Later that night, he was there alone, but the boat was already a considerable distance from land, buffeted by the waves because the wind was against it.
>
> Shortly before dawn Jesus went out to them, walking on the lake. When the disciples saw him walking on the lake, they were terrified. "It's a ghost," they said, and cried out in fear.
>
> But Jesus immediately said to them: "Take courage! It is I. Don't be afraid."[5]

BE BRAVE

With a storm raging and the crew doing everything they could to keep from drowning, suddenly an apparition appeared on the water. Of course, it wasn't a ghost at all but Jesus. Sometimes Jesus is in our line of sight, but our vision is limited in both depth and perception. Our limitations often keep us from truth.

Unaffected, unhindered, and standing in the chaos of the storm, Jesus made three concise statements:

Take courage.

It is I.

Don't be afraid.

You can't "take" courage when it isn't available for the taking.

Courage and the abolishment of fear seem to hinge on three words: IT IS I.

I made this same declaration to my youngest daughter recently while I was out on our back porch taking in the fresh air and dodging the flying insects. Addie appeared at the door, mouthing that she wanted to talk to me. After I motioned for her to join me, she shook her head, indicating she didn't want to because of all the bugs.

"Don't be afraid," I told her. "They're not going to bother you. Take courage! It is I."

She looked at me with a blank stare and then walked away, staying indoors.

Apparently Addie didn't find comfort in "It is I."

It was just me, Dad, and she didn't trust my proficiency in insect swatting.

Have you ever lain in bed at night and felt afraid, even after you locked all your doors and windows? Have you ever spent extra money on tires designed to expertly grip the road in snow and rain, but when faced with adverse driving conditions still felt fearful, wondering if they would do their job?

We apply innumerable contingencies in an attempt to alleviate our fears, but each contingency has its limits. There is only one everlasting place to find true fearlessness: in Jesus.

It is I. The only real security in the universe is in that statement.

And if you can't find security in Him, you'll have trouble finding it anyplace else.

Jesus says to us, "When you know Me, you have no reason to fear. I designed gravity. I control physics. I arranged the number of protons in the nucleus of every chemical element. I have at My command every cycle, every weather pattern, and every organism on the earth itself—in the universe, for that matter."

In other words, He's got you.

FORMULAS OR FAITH

In this account we're presented with a contrast between the boat and the storm.

The boat is safe and secure, comfortable and known. The storm is dark and violent, scary and unknown. You might imagine your boat as that person or thing you trust in place of God. Peter chose to trust God.

> "Lord, if it's you," Peter replied, "tell me to come to you on the water."
>
> "Come," [Jesus] said.
>
> Then Peter got down out of the boat, walked on the water and came toward Jesus.[6]

When confronted with the unfamiliar, many of us choose the boat. We do this over and over because it's safe and predictable.

But what if living by faith isn't optional?

Though we tend to see faith as a one-time thing, it's not. When we fail to walk by faith, we trust the illusion of control.

The more we believe we are in control, the less we think we need God. We hang out with our formulas and boats instead of hanging out with Jesus.

Here's the thing about boats: before you commission one, you have to give it a name.

Draw a boat in the margin of the page and put a name on it.

What's your safety mechanism? Your precious formula? Your unsinkable ship?

Is it ...

Your intellect? Your beauty? Your perfect family? Your emergency fund? Your religion?

The name of my boat is *Organizational Efficiency*. It's my endless struggle. The lie I believe is that if I was just more efficient and could better utilize my time, I would finally conquer my stress and would forever be at peace. Of course, it matters not how organized I am. Over and over God flips my boat, and I'm reminded I cannot control the elements of life.

God loves you and me too much to just let us cruise over calm water throughout our voyage. If He did that, we would drift toward the sunset and forget there's a world around us that He came to restore.

He doesn't want us to give our trust away to an impersonal, abstract god.

Jesus wants to know us. And He wants us to know Him.

ADVERSITY AS OPPORTUNITY

As the boat rocked violently, Peter covered his eyes and squinted through the blinding rain at the solitary figure coming toward him on the water. He took a chance.

Water-walking opportunities don't come around every day.

While the boat was jumping waves, and everyone else was wondering whether the next swell would swamp it, Peter looked through the wind and the waves and yelled, "Lord, if it's you, ... tell me to come."

Jesus then told Peter to put his money where his mouth was.

And in response, Peter stepped over the rail, looked at Jesus, and walked on water. Perhaps you've heard the story and know what happens next: "When [Peter] saw the wind, he was afraid and, beginning to sink, cried out, 'Lord, save me!'"[7]

That night, standing on the water, Peter got distracted. He took his eyes off Jesus and allowed the impossibility of his circumstances to frame his point of view. Suddenly he felt afraid. From euphoria to fright. Terrified that life as he knew it was coming to an end, Peter lost the moment and lost flotation. Collapsing into the waves, he cried out for help.

As you think about this story, remember that all of this happened in the middle of a storm. If you were imagining Jesus' sandals clippity-clapping over the water, reframe your image of the water to include rolling swells and crashing waves. Jesus was probably surfing more than He was walking.

What did Jesus do when Peter began sinking into the churning sea?

> Immediately Jesus reached out his hand and caught him. "You of little faith," he said, "why did you doubt?"

And when they climbed into the boat, the wind died down. Then those who were in the boat worshiped him, saying, "Truly you are the Son of God."[8]

When we finally accept that we aren't in control, we're compelled to boldly recognize who is. Adversity invites obedience.

Human extremity is the frequent meeting place with God.[9]
Dale Bruner

Each time we're thrown into a situation that feels impossible, the first question we're constrained to ask is "Whom do I trust?" In Jesus' simple response to Peter, He was saying with outstretched hand, "Will you trust Me?"

The disciples were in awe of the power and authority of their master. And, of course, they loved Him. But this didn't mean they fully understood or trusted Jesus. We humans need continual reminders. It takes us a while to comprehend truth. Peter and the boys had not yet awakened to life in the Kingdom of God.

How similar are we to Jesus' young followers? What do we not yet understand because we simply have not awakened to His sovereign presence?

In the moments after rescuing Peter, Jesus could have reminded the disciples of His control over gravity, physics, and the number of protons in the nucleus of every chemical element. He could have expounded on His ability to control the water cycle, weather patterns, and every organism on the earth itself. Instead, He climbed into the boat with them.

Isn't God the same way with us? He can always one-up any achievement we claim as our own and show off His power. But showing off seems to be His last resort.

Instead, He comes close.

He sits next to us.

He meets us in our dysfunction.

He walks with us in our lack of awareness.

He calls us to faith.

He calms our storms.

In the chaos and darkness, with a patient and curious tone, Jesus asks each of us, "Do I have the power or don't I? Do you trust My heart? If you don't know Me, you'll probably have trouble trusting Me."

My father once made an interesting observation. He told me that almost every film features the same recurring line. Somewhere in the plot, usually in the rising action, one character looks at another and says, "Trust me."

There is no way to hide from this. It's the centerpiece of every story.

Whom will we trust?

Deep in our souls, this question rings out over every moment of the day.

I believe God whispers back, "Trust Me."

And yet think about how hung up and angry and frazzled and frustrated you can get. Do you not think God has the power to handle the argument you just had with your spouse?

Or next month's rent?

Or your sexual compulsions?

Your inability to follow through?

Your ex-wife?

Your dismissive parents?

Your rebellious children?

The wind and waves that are about to knock over your boat?

Can you find yourself in this story? If so, where are you, and who are you?

Do you relate to Peter?

Are you in a season of confidence, living the impossible and fully trusting God to guide you through the storm? Or are you sinking?

Is your mouth barely above water? Are waves just about to crash over your head?

Are you crying out, "Lord, save me!"?

Maybe you relate to the moment that followed. God has reached out His hand and pulled you from the water, and your confidence in Him now brims with hope and gratitude.

Perhaps you're sitting in the boat, drenched and wet, and those around you who are looking into your story declare with a new recognition, "Wow! Truly there is a God!"

A SURRENDERED LIFE

Peter failed miserably in front of his brother and friends. But let's not forget: he was the only follower who got out of the boat. And he experienced something that no one else in the boat experienced. Perhaps no one else in history.

He walked on water. He defied the laws of nature.

From that day forward, every time he climbed into a vessel on the Sea of Galilee, he would look out at the waves and remember, "I walked on that! Jesus empowered me to do the impossible, just because I asked. Jesus made the impossible possible."

Later in life, Peter became an author. Two of his books are included in the New Testament. In the third chapter of his second book, Peter wrote, "The Lord is not slow in keeping his promise, as some understand slowness. Instead he is patient with you, not wanting anyone to perish, but everyone to come to repentance."[10]

I wonder if Peter paused after he wrote those words, put his head in his hands, and remembered. Perhaps with eyes closed, he tumbled back in time, reliving the suffocating fear of drowning in violent waves, remembering the way Jesus' hand felt around his.

The grip, splashed with seawater but strong.

The loving admonishment, "Why do you doubt?"

Perhaps Peter awakened from his reverie with a whisper: "Lord, I was so young and foolish."

And maybe God whispered back, "Yes, you were, and I loved you then as I do now. You trusted Me, and you were able to defy the natural laws of your earth. Do you yet see what I have in mind for your life? I will use you now to defy the cultural systems of your earth. I have planted you as a seed. From you a movement will grow and spread redemption throughout the world."

Those who live by faith are water walkers. They experience the unusual life because the nature of living by faith is supernatural.

Trust Jesus.

Live the impossible.

What boat is He asking you to leave behind? What water is God calling you to walk out on?

The statements "Take courage," "It is I," and "Don't be afraid" remained with Peter throughout his life. While he wasn't a perfect man—during his ministry he wrestled with the approval of others—the death and resurrection of Jesus and the indwelling of God's Spirit gave him the courage to find his confidence in God. He fearlessly proclaimed the good news of God's love in the heart of the Roman Empire. He was rejected, beaten, and eventually crucified upside down, according to legend, yet the prophetic call of Jesus came true. "You are Peter, and on this rock I will build my church."[11]

Chapter 10

COURAGEOUS CONVICTION

Martin Luther, AD 1483–1546, Germany

Here I stand. I can do no other.

Martin Luther

The team's last supper took place in Rome. Filming for our group's docu-study had come to an end. Everyone but the boys and I was flying out early in the morning. Reflecting on our past two weeks together, we shared the moments that were most memorable and inspiring.

The charm of Paris, the shop-filled streets of Oxford, the solemn beaches of Normandy, Friar Andrew and his Frisbee, and the thousands of steps we must have climbed to inhale the most gorgeous of views were but a few of the memories mentioned around the table. We laughed a lot, cried a little, and continually bathed in the grace of God as we considered the European poets and saints and their impact on our lives.

The next morning the boys and I boarded a train to Annecy, France, where a day later we rented a car and set out on our own adventure. Driving through the Swiss Alps, we were mesmerized. Around each winding turn, we encountered sweeping vistas of seduction. Nursery rhymes and Christmas carols mingled like a serenade in my mind as the enchanting mountainsides and cascading waterfalls beckoned us to take a second and even a third look. We pulled our tiny Renault rental car off the road multiple times to gawk in silence and stare in wonder.

In Austria's Saint Peter's Church cemetery, we reenacted the escape scene filmed in *The Sound of Music* and later trekked to the mountain fortress of Hohensalzburg Castle. In Vienna I took the boys to Saint Charles's Church, or Karlskirche as it's known in Austria, where we listened to the music of Vivaldi, Schubert, and Mozart played on original instruments from the eighteenth century. The rich melodies and celestial compositions left us shaking our heads in reverence and admiration.

We traveled on to the Czech Republic, where we arrived in Prague in time for the six-hundred-year anniversary of the martyrdom of John Hus. Hus was a devoted follower of church Reformer and Oxford theologian John Wycliffe. Hus paid dearly for challenging the Catholic Church. He was burned at the stake, and his followers were disparaged. According to our tour guide, the Czechs still haven't gotten over it, and to this day they hold a general disregard for the church.

Before Hus's ashes were thrown into the Rhine River, his dying words included the following prophetic statement: "In 100 years, God will raise up a man whose calls for reform cannot be suppressed."[1] And in 1517, almost a century later, "Martin Luther nailed his famous 95 Theses of Contention (a list of 95 issues of heretical theology and crimes of the Roman Catholic Church) into the church door at Wittenberg."[2]

Many scholars and historians consider Wittenberg, Germany, the birthplace of the Protestant Reformation, and this was our eventual destination.

THE SHAPING OF A REFORMER

Arriving in Berlin, we met up with my good friend and filmmaker, Jeremy Stanley, who happened to be in Europe at the time. Rather than head home as planned, he graciously agreed to connect with us in the German capital. This was fortuitous, since I'd been planning from the beginning of the trip to film (unrelated to the team) a message in Wittenberg on the life of Martin Luther for our church back home. And while my sons would have been more than willing to shoot the footage with an iPhone, I was pretty sure our congregation would appreciate having a professional cinematographer film the piece.

While the boys settled in for the evening, I reviewed, as was my habit each night, the general itinerary and driving directions for the next day. I was disappointed when my GPS app indicated that Wittenberg wasn't forty-five minutes away, as I had initially thought, but was closer to a four-hour trek. The long drive would significantly limit our time in this historic place. Undaunted, I lay in bed reading about the life of Luther, the student his family pressured to become a lawyer, who instead turned monk then priest then professor, and ultimately was responsible for starting a revolution.

Interestingly enough, that was never what he set out to do.

Born in 1483, Luther grew up in a harsh household in Mansfeld, Germany. His father, a successful miner who eventually owned the mines he once worked, was demanding in his expectations and quite severe with his punishments. Here again we discover another poet with a father wound. Similarly, Luther's teachers were known for the severity of their reprimands. This greatly influenced Luther throughout his life, as he formed a habit of resisting dominant, power-over, abusive leadership structures. Like Saint Francis's father, Luther's dad expected a lot from his son and set aside money for the big plans he had for his son's future.

One night while Luther was on his way to the university where he was a law student, he got caught in a violent thunderstorm. When lightning struck nearby, he fell to the ground in terror and vowed to Saint Anna that if God would rescue him from this tempest, he would dedicate his life in service to Him. This vow was perhaps a timely opportunity to evade his father's vicarious plans. Abandoning his studies at law school, Luther became a monk and joined an Augustinian friary in Erfurt, Germany.

Luther's story indicates that he was an intense individual. Fiercely bent on upholding the truth, he did whatever his religious superiors asked him to do. This passion, however, kindled an internal challenge. Having a heightened awareness of his own sin, Luther was consumed with the conflict between caving to selfishness and being obedient to his Lord. In his room late at night, he could be overheard alternately screaming at Satan and then crying out to God. After exiting a confession booth where he'd just confessed his sins, Luther would often turn right around and step back in to confess another sin he had just remembered.

Luther was disoriented, unable to grasp how he would ever be able to display enough penance to move forward in serving God. The crushing weight of serving a "just" God who demanded perfection from him was terrifying. Why serve a God who was a divine reflection of his father and other early authority figures? Luther realized as a monk that his commitment to follow God wasn't grounded in love: it had been constructed by hate.

He hated God.

And it took everything within him to keep from hating the church.

Penance, in particular, angered Luther. Penance is the practice in which those in the church confess their sins to a superior authority to receive forgiveness. The priest, or church official, then identifies what the parishioner needs to do to atone for his or her sins (e.g., give money, perform acts of service, repeat a certain prayer a certain number of times, or engage in some type of self-punishment). To Luther, this system of faith that relied on a middleman and required deeds to express repentance and receive forgiveness prevented believers from directly accessing the grace of God.

In the midst of Luther's internal struggles, his confessor, also considered his spiritual father, sent him on a pilgrimage to Rome. For an idealistic monk, this wasn't a good year to visit the Italian city. The church was in the middle of building Saint Peter's Basilica (yes, the one from the previous chapter) and needed to raise a lot of money fast. The pope in power, Pope Leo X, was said to be a corrupt and manipulative leader. He was a hustler who used papal products, such as indulgences—declarations from the church that remitted a person from purgatory. He recruited a man named Johann Tetzel to travel into the heart of Germany and fleece the people of their money through fear and intimidation.

Like a huckster selling snake oil, Tetzel advised unsuspecting churchgoers that if they put a coin in the offering box, one of their loved ones would be released from his or her temporary state of death. He attempted to motivate Christians by playing on superstitions and using gimmicky slogans like "As soon as the coin in the coffer rings, the soul from purgatory springs."[3]

The church became distracted and lost its true sense of the gospel. Note that when I say *church*, I'm talking about the hierarchy and structure of the dynasty created by the Roman Catholic Church at that time. This isn't an indictment on modern-day Catholicism but rather a review of where the church was during that period of history. While there were some exceptions, most of those at the top of this hierarchy had become corrupted by power and greed.

Witnessing this in Rome firsthand, Luther returned to Germany disillusioned by the very church leadership he had pledged to serve. Not shying away from Luther's apprehension, his confessor sent him to become a pastor and teacher of Scripture at the newly established University of Wittenberg. There, Luther began to study the book of Romans with great diligence. When he was thirty-two years old, he concluded that the Bible taught something that was contrary to his experience.

There is no one righteous, not even one; there is no one who understands; there is no one who seeks God.[4]

Paul the apostle

The church had taught Luther that the justice of God was aimed at inflicting punishment on sinners. The only way to counter this was to become righteous, and this left Luther in a constant state of frustration, since he could never become righteous enough. Reflecting on his first Mass, Luther wrote, "I was utterly stupefied and terror-stricken. I thought to myself, 'Who am I that I should lift up mine eyes or raise my hands to the divine majesty? For I am dust and ashes and full of sin, and I am speaking to the living, eternal and true God.'"[5]

While studying the Pauline letter, Luther began to understand that it was the death, resurrection, and redemption of Jesus that imputed upon humankind a righteousness that would satisfy the demands of a holy God.

No one will be declared righteous in God's sight by the works of the law; rather, through the law we become conscious of our sin.

But now apart from the law the righteousness of God has been made known, to which the Law and the Prophets testify. This righteousness is given through faith in Jesus Christ to all who believe. There is no difference between Jew and Gentile, for all have sinned and fall short of the glory of God, and all are justified freely by his grace through the redemption that came by Christ Jesus.[6]

From Luther's perspective, both faith and righteousness were free gifts given to repentant sinners. If it were true that salvation came through faith in Christ alone, the roles of intercessors were no longer necessary.

These revelations drastically changed his view of God. Rather than seeing God as a divine entity ever angry with His creation, Luther began to know Him as a kind, loving, and holy being who chose to love humanity in the midst of its rebellion.

Continuing in his pastoral duties and his teaching at the university, Luther slowly began to gather colleagues to his new way of thinking. And he began to write. Luther challenged the practice of selling indulgences in *Ninety-Five Theses on the Power and Efficacy of Indulgences*, which are known today as Luther's Ninety-Five Theses.

Thesis 32 displays Luther's passionate challenge to the unscrupulous exploitation of indulgences:

> Those who suppose that on account of their letters of indulgence they are sure of salvation will be eternally damned along with their teachers.[7]

And Thesis 51 is a prime example of how direct and concise Luther could be as he challenged the building of Saint Peter's Basilica:

> Christians should be taught that the pope ought and would give his own substance to the poor, from whom certain preachers of indulgences extract money, even if he had to sell St. Peter's Cathedral to do it.[8]

While there is some discrepancy, legend has it that like posting a blog, Luther nailed his theses to the door of the Castle Church in Wittenberg in hopes that others would consider his point of view. Luther didn't grasp the implications of his bold arguments. He wasn't looking for a rebellion. Nor did he want to create a whole new way of doing church. Luther simply wanted reform.

THE ROAD TO WITTENBERG

The sky was overcast as I double-checked and confirmed our travel route, and Jeremy, the boys, and I set out on our four-hour drive to

Wittenberg. Our rental car was small. Adding a fourth person forced us to cram our luggage into every available crevice.

Jeremy has brown hair, brown eyes, and a full beard. Apparently the combination of a car full of luggage and a Middle Eastern–looking man wasn't a good one.

The following day while we were driving in France, a French policeman waved us down. With his arm gesturing out the window, he motioned for us to follow him. Bewildered and a bit reluctant, I obliged. Several miles later we pulled off the highway and into the lot of an abandoned construction site. While my slow-moving tires crunched the gravel beneath us, Jeremy muttered under his breath, "What in the world is happening?"

The police car in front of us came to a stop, and from out of nowhere, six other officers appeared, their faces threatening, hands placed firmly on their weapons.

At this point I engaged the accent I learned while living in the South and attempted to make myself sound very American. As I rolled down the window, I asked if there was a problem.

The unamused police officer ignored my question. In his thick French accent, he asked what we were doing in France. I responded that we were studying church history.

He glanced back at his stern-faced colleagues and smirked, saying something in French about our being Americans.

Apparently viewing us as nonthreats and unworthy of official police business, the officer told us he was done with us. He was kind enough, however, to motion us in the direction of the highway.

But that little incident happened the next day.

Our adventure in Germany was just unfolding. Arriving in Witttenberg around noon, we drove slowly down narrow cobblestone streets, taking in the tranquil, little German town as we sought our destination, Castle Church. Framed in painted timber and red brick, the houses had a timeless quality about them. As we rambled up and down unusually quiet streets, we realized we had a problem.

There was no Castle Church.

There was nothing referencing Martin Luther at all.

After taking several more laps through this motionless town, an awful feeling of trepidation came over me, the kind where it feels as though your stomach drops through your legs and onto the floor.

Temporarily setting aside my focus on finding the Castle Church, I took in the oddity of our surroundings. The town seemed deserted. *Where is everyone?* The streets were lined with shops and storefronts, but there was no observable activity in or around them. And this was the middle of the day. I would have thought the place would be buzzing with people milling about, walking, socializing, shopping, selling—something! But there was no movement whatsoever. It was as if we had entered the Twilight Zone. Dumbfounded, I gripped the wheel as the Renault crawled along, and Jeremy and the boys started making comments about the onset of a zombie apocalypse.

Then, a human being.

We pulled up to a postal worker placing a parcel in a mailbox. I rolled down the window and said, "Excuse me, can you point us to the Castle Church?"

The German woman looked at me blankly.

Hearing the guys continue doling out apocalyptic comments, I started to sweat. A bit disoriented, I almost hit the woman while pulling away. Jeremy joked, "Hey, you don't have to drive over the woman just because she doesn't speak English!" Mocking me, he chided, "Excuse me, ma'am, you don't speak English? Please step in front of the car."

I apologized for my disorientation, and we all started laughing. But secretly I was a little worried. "Gentlemen. Where are we?"

We finally found a building that looked like a travel agency and pulled up to seek directions. It was closed. A middle-aged woman with a pale complexion pulled up in a car even smaller than ours and parked alongside. "Excuse me, ma'am. Can you direct us to anything involving Martin Luther?"

Another blank stare.

I tried an alternative. "Can you direct us to the tourist center?" With a look of terror, she shook her head and said something in German that I interpreted to mean "I don't know English, and I don't know you. Please leave." Now it was getting weird.

The pain of the moment started bearing down on me. Then it hit me. "Guys," I blurted out sheepishly, "we're in the wrong Wittenberg!!"

Sure enough, there are two Wittenbergs in Germany, and we were in the wrong one. The one spelled Wittenb-u-r-g.

MEDIEVAL MEDIA

Driving away more than a little despondent, I gradually began to accept reality. For a brief minute, we considered making the trek back to the Wittenberg I longed for, but we realized that in doing so we would have to forfeit the remainder of our itinerary.

I was disappointed. But the frustration I felt over my GPS misleading me was a far cry from the frustration the German people must have felt when the church, the very institution they were meant to trust, continually took advantage of them.

When Luther's theses were made public, someone, perhaps a college student, felt so validated that he threw himself into the task of disseminating the information through the social media of his day. *The Economist* tells the story this way:

> In December 1517 printed editions of the theses, in the form of pamphlets and broadsheets, appeared simultaneously in Leipzig, Nuremberg and Basel, paid for by Luther's friends to whom he had sent copies. German translations, which could be read by a wider public than Latin-speaking academics and clergy, soon followed and quickly spread throughout the German-speaking lands. Luther's friend Friedrich Myconius later wrote that "hardly 14 days had passed when these propositions were known throughout Germany and within four weeks almost all of Christendom was familiar with them.[9]

For the first time in religious history, the power of social media in pamphlet form changed the world.

Validation.

Solidarity.

Luther's challenge empowered the masses to resist the powerful.

Have you ever read a blog or listened to a communicator put into words something you had been feeling—perhaps for years—and experienced an overwhelming sense of satisfaction? Your belief in that moment found validation. You were no longer alone in your conviction. In that moment you found solidarity.

That was exactly what happened in the hearts of the German people. Across the country peasants began to rise up in opposition to the political and religious forces that sought to control them. Mix in an economic crisis, an impending Muslim invasion, and political upheaval, and you have the recipe for a revolution.

In 1521, four years after Luther's theses had been circulating, and with the balance of power at stake, church officials and German royalty gathered in the city of Worms and took Luther to trial. An inquisitor, standing with Luther's pamphlets and books on display in front of him, asked the Reformer if he believed what he wrote.

Luther struggled to answer. Remember, he didn't want to run from the church; he wanted to reform it. After being granted a day to consider his answer, Luther returned to his trial and spoke with confidence: "Unless I am convinced by proofs from Scriptures or by plain and clear reasons and arguments, I can and will not retract, for it is neither safe nor wise to do anything against conscience."[10]

According to tradition, Luther's final words reverberated throughout history:

"Here I stand, I can do no other. God help me."[11]

It's not accidental that Luther summoned the mercy of God. He wasn't just defying a local church; he was defying the imperial ruling entity of Europe. For his admission, Luther would likely be condemned and executed. Beyond a doubt, this man exemplified courage. In the face of almost certain death, Luther claimed the primacy of conscience over political expediency. He defied the corruption in the church and upheld the rights of the individual to claim a direct relationship with God.

Luther offered invigorating answers to the questions of faith and forgiveness. And while he was one of many voices of reform that would sweep through Europe, "Luther stands symbolically as the greatest single agent in increasing the value of the individual. What eventually emerges (although it took two more centuries and couldn't have happened without the Enlightenment) is a new kind of individual. That made democratic government possible."[12]

John Calvin would not have been able to shape his ideals of government had Luther not paved the way. The ripple effect of Luther's life continues to reverberate throughout history.

FIERCE INTENTIONALITY

Considering Luther's story and his deep conviction, I'm forced to ask myself, "What am I not okay with in my culture?"

- I'm not okay with men and women being trafficked, their spirits crushed and their dignity violently ripped from their being.

- I'm not okay with children being abandoned or forced to murder other human beings.
- And closer to my doorstep, I'm not okay with the holy and just, gracious and loving message of Jesus being used as a club to dominate and manipulate the unsuspecting.

I've sat with hundreds of people who have been abused in religious systems where those in leadership wielded their spiritual authority to further personal and godless agendas.

As a pastor, I'll be the first to confess that when someone in leadership casts a vision for a church, there is no way to extract that person from the vision. While in every way my goal is to be objective and healthily detached from my congregation, I'm unable to separate myself from myself. My personality *is* stamped on the church I serve, along with David's, Leslie's, Sarah's, and a host of others, since our personalities are imprinted on our DNA.

This doesn't seem inconsistent with Scripture. God uses all kinds of personalities, and it's evident that they leave their marks on the people they serve.

The real issue isn't whether a church is flavored with its leaders' personalities but whether church leaders are attempting to use the name of God to build their own personal kingdoms. In this adulterated system, the congregation lives like a parasite off the firsthand experiences of its leaders. We're each invited into relationship with

God. We're each called to do the work of discovering the gifts He has placed within us and offering those gifts back to Him as an act of worship. It is the variety of our gifts and the diversity of our callings that set us apart, make us unique, and allow us to participate in a significant way in Kingdom work.

Just as a body, though one, has many parts, but all its many parts form one body, so it is with Christ. For we were all baptized by one Spirit so as to form one body—whether Jews or Gentiles, slave or free—and we were all given the one Spirit to drink. Even so the body is not made up of one part but of many.[13]

On a similar note, because I'm passionate about releasing people to their God-given designs, I'm not okay with followers of Jesus squandering their lives, wandering aimlessly in their lethargy, failing to awaken the beauty within. Each of us is created in the image of God and has a gift we're meant to give the world. I long to see organizational systems in place where people are loved and released to express their giftedness.

What about you?

What are you not okay with?

Whom are you willing to oppose?

What are you so passionate about that you would be willing to face rejection, even execution?

Where in your life is there fierce intentionality?

LEGACY

It's difficult to fully grasp Martin Luther's far-reaching contribution to the human experience. Along with igniting the spark of the Reformation, he helped lay the foundation for modern education in his country. By translating the Latin Bible into the German vernacular, he provided a reference point for a common German language.

With great irony, Luther, a former monk, eventually married a former nun. And they had six kids! By teaching his children to connect with their consciences, they developed an ability to listen to the Holy Spirit as they studied the Holy Scriptures. Educated and empowered by the grace of God, many of them and future generations carried on Luther's work in the ministry.

I know this to be true because on one particular Sunday after I mentioned this great Reformer in a talk at church, a woman named Lynette introduced herself to me as a direct descendant of Martin Luther. After stammering a bit, I communicated my astonishment and curiosity. We got together a few weeks later, at which point she showed me her family tree and the prolific number of family members who served the Lord faithfully, carrying Luther's message through the generations.

It's important to note that Luther's historical legacy isn't without blemish.

In his later years he was churlish and coarse. He carried prejudices, in particular an anti-Semitic bias that Adolf Hitler exploited and embellished four hundred years later. While his context and his reaction to a time of turmoil in Germany called the Peasants' Revolt deeply affected Luther's writings about the Jewish people, we wouldn't describe every aspect of his life as saint-like.

As I observed earlier, while some in the Christian community call various men and women saints, it's not because they were perfect; it's because they are remembered for the way they dedicated their lives to God. No saint is without struggle. Each has wrestled with his or her own tragic impairments.

Throughout his life, Luther continued to work out the pain of his childhood. Though he was a man who influenced all of history, he struggled with bouts of depression, counting on his community and family to pull him through the fog.

We need each other.

We need perspective.

HOW BIG IS YOUR GOD?

We have a tendency to make God out to be the best version of ourselves. When we struggle with the image or character of God, it's because He's so tiny in our frame. But He is massive, both just and merciful. Our frame cannot contain His glory.

Our fall from that great glory and our resulting sinful nature shifts our gaze. And sin is grotesque. We must feel the weight of it.

The intensity of our sin actually helps us understand the significance of God's redemption. If our sin is just a casual thing, something to shrug off, then what's the importance of God's grace? The depth and passion of His love is connected to the fallenness of our sin nature. Luther got that. And he helped the church see it in a whole different light.

How immense is God?

How well do we know Him?

Do we put Him on a leash and walk Him around, occasionally calling out commands and offering Him special treats?

Or is He an immeasurably powerful entity beyond our wildest imaginations?

Luther wrote that God's highest form of self-disclosure takes place on the cross of Christ. There He is seen in weakness and suffering and as a stumbling block that stands in the way of humanity's preconceived notions of divine glory.

The cross: God's personal reveal.

Do our lives reflect this kind of conviction?

Is this how we surrender our preferences, our conveniences, and our lust for acknowledgment?

If you're wondering how you might do that, here are some suggestions:

- Stare pride and the royal quest for glory dead in the eye and dethrone it.
- Tell someone you're sorry.
- Ask for forgiveness.
- Compliment the person you envy most.
- Give up your parking space.
- Clean off a table without being asked.
- Sacrifice something for someone.

When we choose Christ, we choose to feel the pain that is associated with the death of the ego. We let go of our presumed rights. We surrender our wills. His divine light illuminates something within us. His divine presence eviscerates the old self that stands in the way.

Our eyes sting as we awaken and grow accustomed to the beauty.

The fullness of life is seared on our hearts, and the healing salve is fully applied only when we exit this world and join Him in the next.

This is why the funeral of a believer is such a celebration. The child of God finally arrives home, where his or her joy is made complete.

James K. A. Smith writes, "Our identity is shaped by what we ultimately love or what we love as ultimate—what, at the end of the day, gives us a sense of meaning, purpose, understanding, and orientation to our being-in-the-world."[14]

What or whom exists in your life as your ultimate love?

What orients you to being in the world?

Who gives your life meaning?

"What makes us who we are, the kind of people we are—is what [and whom] we love."[15]

EPILOGUE

"William Stafford was once asked in an interview, 'When did you decide to be a poet?' He responded that the question was put wrongly: everyone is born a poet—a person discovering the way words sound and work, caring and delighting in words. I just kept on doing, he said, what everyone starts out doing. 'The real question is why did the other people stop?'"[1]

While traveling with my family in Nicaragua a few years back, our host took us to an artisan's shop where a man named George Zappada made guitars.

Each guitar was handcrafted, carved from wood.

Each guitar was unique.

Each one had its own shape and designs.

Each one had its own sound.

The imprint of the designer, his signature and personality, was pressed into each guitar.

> Each being on earth is such [an instrument], and each of us releases our song when Spirit passes through the holes carved by our experience.... Since no two [instruments] have the same holes, no two [instruments] make the same music.... And no two beings sing the same song, for the holes in each life produce their own unrepeatable melody.
>
> There is a great ongoing choice that awaits us each and every day: whether we go around carving holes in others because we've been so painfully carved, or whether we let Spirit play its song through our tender experience, enabling us to listen to the miraculous music coming through others.... We carve and cry when it is we who are carved in order that we may sing.[2]

It wasn't until after the faith of these poets and saints was tested and their pride was crushed that the melodies of Jesus' love could flow from them. It's the same with us.

That hole in your heart can either continue to bleed, or it can become the place where the song of your life is heard. The world desperately needs you to be who you are.

Why?

You are handcrafted.

You have felt the blade—cuts from another, self-inflicted wounds—but the chisel of the Carpenter reforms and redeems. He takes what would otherwise be distorted and makes you beautiful.

You are unique.

You have your own sound, your own shape.

You carry the imprint of your designer; His signature and personality are pressed into your soul. Chiseling. Repairing. Restoring.

He sets you on display for the world to see. For you are His pride and joy.

You have suffered, but your suffering has purpose. In the meal you cook, in the email you type, in the sale you make, or in the smile you give, allow the poetry of your soul the freedom of expression.

Live on, saint. You have a song to sing.

NOTES

CHAPTER 1: MAY LOVE FIND US

1. Thomas Cahill, *How the Irish Saved Civilization* (New York: Anchor Books, 1995), 108.

2. Saint Patrick, "Saint Patrick's *Confessio*," trans. Pádraig McCarthy, 2003, sec. 16, accessed May 13, 2016, www.confessio.ie/etexts/confessio_english#.

3. *Confessio*, sec. 2.

4. Abraham Joshua Heschel, *I Asked for Wonder: A Spiritual Anthology* (New York: Crossroad, 1987), 3.

5. Saint Patrick, *The Confession of St. Patrick*, Christian Classics Ethereal Library, sec. 17, accessed May 13, 2016, www.ccel.org/ccel/patrick/confession.v.html.

6. Philip Yancey, *Vanishing Grace: Whatever Happened to the Good News?* (Grand Rapids: Zondervan, 2014), 57.

7. Miranda Green, *Symbol and Image in Celtic Religious Art* (New York: Routledge, 1992), 174.

8. Mark Buchanan, *The Holy Wild: Trusting in the Character of God* (Colorado Springs: Multnomah, 2003), 84.

9. Cahill, *How the Irish Saved Civilization*, 115.

10. John Finney, *Recovering the Past: Celtic and Roman Mission* (London: Darton, Longman, and Todd, 1996), summarized in George G. Hunter, *The Celtic Way of Evangelism* (Nashville: Abingdon Press, 2010), 42–43.

11. First Corinthians 9:19–23 THE MESSAGE.

12. Saint Patrick, "Saint Patrick's *Confessio*," sec. 1.

13. Cahill, *How the Irish Saved Civilization*, iii.

14. Ephesians 4:11–12 NKJV.

15. Saint Patrick, "Lorica of Saint Patrick," ETWN.com, accessed May 10, 2016, www.ewtn.com/Devotionals/prayers/patrick.htm.

CHAPTER 2: EMBRACE YOUR LIMITATIONS

1. William Cowper, quoted in Alexander Campbell, *The Millennial Harbinger* (Bethany, VA: A. Campbell, 1852), 2:228.

2. James 2:26 NKJV.

3. Erwin R. McManus, *The Artisan Soul: Crafting Your Life into a Work of Art* (New York: HarperOne, 2015), 145–46.

4. McManus, *The Artisan Soul*, 146.

5. Brené Brown, *The Gifts of Imperfection: Let Go of Who You Think You're Supposed to Be and Embrace Who You Are* (Center City, MN: Hazelden, 2010), 96.

6. Henri Nouwen, *The Wounded Healer: Ministry in Contemporary Society* (New York: Doubleday, 1972), 38.

CHAPTER 3: TO BE SEEN AND KNOWN

1. C. S. Lewis, *Surprised by Joy: The Shape of My Early Life* (New York: Harcourt Brace, 1955), 206.

2. Lewis, *Surprised by Joy*, 221.

3. C. S. Lewis, *A Grief Observed* (New York: HarperCollins, 1961), 52.

4. J. R. R. Tolkien, *The Lord of the Rings*, 50th Anniversary Edition (Great Britain: HarperCollins, 2004), 51.

5. C. S. Lewis, *The Four Loves: The Much Beloved Exploration of the Nature of Love* (New York: Mariner Books, 1971), 59.

6. W. H. Lewis, "Memoir of C. S. Lewis," in C. S. Lewis, *Letters of C. S. Lewis*, ed. W. H. Lewis, rev. Harvest ed. (Orlando, FL: Harcourt, 1993), 34.

7. Michael Dirda, "'The Fellowship' Explores the Spiritual Roots of Tolkien and the Inklings," *Washington Post*, July 1, 2015, www.washingtonpost.com/entertainment/books/the-fellowship-explores-the-spiritual-roots-of-tolkien-and-the-inklings/2015/07/01/79ac6744-1c21-11e5-ab92-c75ae6ab94b5_story.html.

8. C. S. Lewis, *Till We Have Faces* (New York: Harcourt Brace, 1980), 294.

9. Brené Brown, *The Gifts of Imperfection* (Center City, MN: Hazelden, 2010), 26.

10. Ephesians 2:10.

11. John Ortberg, *The Me I Want to Be: Becoming God's Best Version of You* (Grand Rapids: Zondervan, 2010), 15.

12. C. S. Lewis, *The Lion, the Witch and the Wardrobe* (New York: Macmillan, 1950), 160–61.

CHAPTER 4: EVERY MOMENT IS A GIFT

1. "Orthodoxologist," *Time*, October 11, 1943.

2. G. K. Chesterton, quoted in Stephen Prickett, *Victorian Fantasy*, 2nd ed. (Waco, TX: Baylor University Press, 2005), 254n68.

3. C. S. Lewis, *George MacDonald: An Anthology; 365 Readings* (New York: HarperCollins, 2015), xxiii.

4. George MacDonald, *Paul Faber, Surgeon* (Philadelphia: J. B. Lippincott, 1879), 100.

5. See Matthew 20:16.

6. Lewis, *George MacDonald*, xxvi.

7. C. S. Lewis, *Surprised by Joy: The Shape of My Early Life* (New York: Harcourt Brace, 1955), 179–80.

8. Ecclesiastes 1:9.

9. Timothy Keller, *Every Good Endeavor: Connecting Your Work to God's Work* (New York: Dutton, 2012), 29–30.

10. Lewis, *George MacDonald*, 3.

11. Lewis, *George MacDonald*, xxviii.

12. George MacDonald, *"Beautiful Thoughts"* (New York: James Pott, 1894), 19.

13. Ephesians 1:3–6 THE MESSAGE.

14. Richard Rohr, *Things Hidden: Scripture as Spirituality* (Cincinnati: St. Anthony Messenger Press, 2007), 35.

15. Luke 1:26–38.

CHAPTER 5: OUR HEARTS ARE MADE FOR LOVE

1. Ronald Rolheiser, *Against an Infinite Horizon: The Finger of God in Our Everyday Lives* (New York: Crossroad, 2001), 152–53.

2. "Her Life at Lisieux Carmel," Society of the Little Flower, www.littleflower.org /therese/life-story/her-life-at-lisieux-carmel/.

3. "Her Life at Lisieux Carmel."

4. Matthew 19:14.

5. Saint Thérèse of Lisieux, *The Story of the Soul: The Autobiography of St. Therese of Lisieux*, trans. Thomas N. Taylor (New York: Cosimo, 2007), 121, 122.

6. Saint Thérèse of Lisieux, quoted in Glenn F. Chesnut, *God and Spirituality: Philosophical Essays* (Bloomington, IN: iUniverse, 2010), 317.

7. First John 3:16–20 THE MESSAGE.

8. Abraham Joshua Heschel, *I Asked for Wonder: A Spiritual Anthology* (New York: Crossroad, 1987), 3.

9. First Corinthians 13:1.

10. First Corinthians 13:4–6.

11. First Corinthians 13:6–8.

12. Rob Bell, *Sex God: Exploring the Endless Connections between Sexuality and Spirituality* (New York: HarperOne, 2012), 62.

13. Saint Thérèse of Lisieux, *The Story of the Soul*, 92.

14. Dr. Keith Ablow, "Was Jesus the First Psychiatrist?" "Fox News Opinion," FoxNews.com, September 23, 2011, www.foxnews.com/opinion/2011/09/23/what-do-jesus-psychology-and-psychiatry-have-in-common.html.

15. Saint Thérèse of Lisieux, *The Story of the Soul*, 63.

INTERLUDE: THE VOICE OF ARCHITECTURE

1. Alain de Botton, *The Architecture of Happiness* (New York: Vintage, 2008), 112.

2. *Inside Out*, directed by Pete Docter and Ronnie Del Carmen (Burbank, CA: Walt Disney Pictures, 2015).

3. Botton, *Architecture of Happiness*, 147.

4. Matthew 5:4.

CHAPTER 6: THE PERSONAL GOD

1. Peter Steinfels, "Man of Contradictions, Shaper of Modernity. Age? 500 Next Week," *New York Times*, July 3, 2009, www.nytimes.com/2009/07/04/us/04beliefs.html?pagewanted=1&_r=3.

2. Doug Phillips, "John Calvin, Founding Father," Faithstreet.com, July 7, 2009, accessed May 10, 2016, www.faithstreet.com/onfaith/2009/07/07/the-calvin-quincentenary-and-american-liberty/6929.

3. Justo L. González, *The Story of Christianity*, vol. 2, *The Reformation to the Present Day*, 2nd ed. (New York: HarperOne, 2010), 81.

4. John Calvin, preface to 1542 *Geneva Psalter*, quoted in Philip E. Stoltzfus, *Theology as Performance: Music, Aesthetics, and God in Modern Theology* (New York: T & T Clark, 2006), 44.

5. Larry Crabb, *Finding God* (Grand Rapids: Zondervan, 1995), 29n.

6. Frank Viola, "Shocking Beliefs of John Calvin," *The Deeper Journey* (blog), Patheos.com, April 8, 2015, www.patheos.com/blogs/frankviola /shockingbeliefsofjohncalvin/.

7. Viola, "Shocking Beliefs."

8. Eugene H. Peterson, *Tell It Slant: A Conversation on the Language of Jesus in His Stories and Prayers* (Grand Rapids: Eerdmans, 2008), 60.

9. Luke 2:10–12.

10. Peterson, *Tell It Slant*, 60.

11. Peterson, *Tell It Slant*, 61.

12. Joshua 24:15.

CHAPTER 7: CREATED FOR MORE

1. Mark DeVries and Kirk Freeman, eds., *Augustine's Confessions* (Nashville: B&H Publishing Group, 1998), 15.

2. Augustine, *Confessions*, 37.

3. Augustine, *Confessions*, 37.

4. Augustine, quoted in Robin Lane Fox, *Augustine, Conversions to Confessions* (New York: Basic Books, 2015), 82.

5. Fox, *Augustine*, 85, 87.

6. Gerald G. May, *The Wisdom of Wilderness: Experiencing the Healing Power of Nature* (New York: HarperCollins, 2006), 10.

7. May, *The Wisdom of Wilderness*, 13.

8. Ecclesiastes 3:11.

9. C. S. Lewis, *Mere Christianity*, rev. ed. (New York: HarperCollins, 1980), 136–37.

10. Second Corinthians 3:6.

11. Peter Brown, *Augustine of Hippo: A Biography* (Berkeley, CA: University of California Press, 2000), 101.

12. Paul R. Spickard and Kevin M. Cragg, *A Global History of Christians: How Everyday Believers Experienced Their World* (Grand Rapids: Baker Academic, 1994), 62.

13. Saint Augustine, *The Confessions of Saint Augustine*, trans. Edward B. Pusey, Christian Classics Ethereal Library, bk. 9, chap. xii, www.ccel.org/ccel /augustine/confess.x.xii.html.

14. Justo L. Gonzalez, *The Story of Christianity*, vol. 1, *The Early Church to the Dawn of the Reformation*, rev. ed. (New York: HarperOne, 2010), 247.

15. Saint Augustine, quoted in John Calvin, *Institutes of the Christian Religion*, ed. John T. McNeill, trans. Ford Lewis Battles, (Louisville, KY: Westminster John Knox Press, 2006), 265.

16. Saint Augustine, *The City of God*, trans. Marcus Dods (London: Catholic Way Publishing, 2015), 429.

17. N. T. Wright, *Simply Christian: Why Christianity Makes Sense* (New York: HarperOne, 2010), 209 (emphasis added).

18. Richard Rohr, *Things Hidden: Scripture as Spirituality* (Cincinnati: St. Anthony Messenger Press, 2007), 17.

19. Timothy Keller, *The Meaning of Marriage: Facing the Complexities of Commitment with the Wisdom of God*, with Kathy Keller (New York: Riverhead Books, 2011), 44.

20. Keller, *Meaning of Marriage*, 44.

21. Rohr, *Things Hidden*, 16.

22. Gonzalez, *The Story of Christianity*, 250.

23. Matthew 25:34.

24. I. Lilias Trotter, *Parables of the Cross* (New York: Start Publishing, 2012), 1.

25. John 11:40.

CHAPTER 8: THE WAY OF HUMILITY

1. Gerald G. May, *The Wisdom of Wilderness: Experiencing the Healing Power of Nature* (New York: HarperCollins, 2006), xx.

2. G. K. Chesterson, *St. Francis of Assisi* (Mineola, NY: Dover, 2008), 133.

3. Robert West, *Saint Francis* (Nashville: Thomas Nelson, 2010), 30.

4. John Eldredge, *Wild at Heart: Discovering the Secret of a Man's Soul*, rev. ed. (Nashville: Thomas Nelson, 2010), 9–10.

5. West, *Saint Francis*, 51.

6. Ronald Rolheiser, *Against an Infinite Horizon: The Finger of God in Our Everyday Lives* (New York: Crossroad, 2001), 57.

7. West, *Saint Francis*, 68.

8. Author's words, based on the story in West, *Saint Francis*.

9. Regis J. Armstrong, J. A. Wayne Hellmann, and William J. Short, eds., *Francis of Assisi: Early Documents*, vol. 2, *The Founder* (New York: New City Press, 2000), 78.

10. Brent Curtis and John Eldredge, *The Sacred Romance: Drawing Closer to the Heart of God* (Nashville: Thomas Nelson, 1997), 7.

11. West, *Saint Francis*, 76.

12. Matthew 13:44–46.

13. West, *Saint Francis*, 80.

14. Anthony De Mello, *The Way to Love: Meditations for Life* (New York: Image, 1992), 26–27, 66.

15. West, *Saint Francis*, 103.

16. Rolheiser, *Against an Infinite Horizon*, 44.

17. Francis of Assisi, "All Creatures of Our God and King," trans. William H. Draper, public domain. Saint Francis penned the original poem, "Canticle of the Sun," in 1225.

CHAPTER 9: LIVE THE IMPOSSIBLE

1. First Peter 5:6.

2. John 1:40–42.

3. Matthew 16:18.

4. Matthew 14:22.

5. Matthew 14:23–27.

6. Matthew 14:28–29.

7. Matthew 14:30.

8. Matthew 14:31–33.

9. Dale Bruner, quoted in John Ortberg, *If You Want to Walk on Water, You've Got to Get Out of the Boat* (Grand Rapids, MI: Zondervan, 2008), 8.

10. Second Peter 3:9.

11. Matthew 16:18.

CHAPTER 10: COURAGEOUS CONVICTION

1. John Hus, quoted in "English Bible History: John Hus," Greatsite.com, accessed May 13, 2016, www.greatsite.com/timeline-english-bible-history/john-hus.html.

2. "English Bible History: John Hus."

3. Johann Tetzel, quoted in Bruce L. Shelley, *Church History in Plain Language*, 4th ed. (Nashville: Thomas Nelson, 2013), 250.

4. Romans 3:10–11.

5. Martin Luther, quoted in Shelley, *Church History in Plain Language*, 248.

6. Romans 3:20–24.

7. "Protestants' Most-Famous Document," "Christian History," ChristianityToday.com, accessed May 13, 2016, www.christianitytoday.com/history/issues/issue-34 /protestants-most-famous-document.html.

8. "Protestants' Most-Famous Document."

9. "How Luther Went Viral," *Economist*, December 17, 2011, www.economist.com /node/21541719.

10. Martin Luther, quoted in "English Bible History: Martin Luther," GreatSite.com, accessed May 13, 2016, www.greatsite.com/timeline-english-bible-history /martin-luther.html.

11. Martin Luther, quoted in "English Bible History: Martin Luther."

12. Martin E. Marty, "Luther's Living Legacy," interview by Christian History Institute, in *Christian History*, no. 39 (1993), www.christianhistoryinstitute.org /magazine/article/luthers-living-legacy/.

13. First Corinthians 12:12–14.

14. James K. A. Smith, *Desiring the Kingdom: Worship, Worldview, and Cultural Formation* (Grand Rapids: Baker Academic, 2009), 26–27.

15. Smith, *Desiring the Kingdom*, 26.

EPILOGUE

1. Eugene Peterson, *Run with the Horses: The Quest for Life at Its Best* (Downers Grove, IL: InterVarsity, 2009), 31.

2. Mark Nepo, *As Far as the Heart Can See: Stories to Illuminate the Soul* (Deerfield Beach, Florida: HCI, 2011), 78–79.

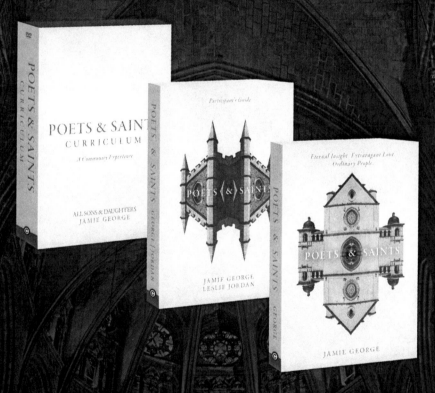

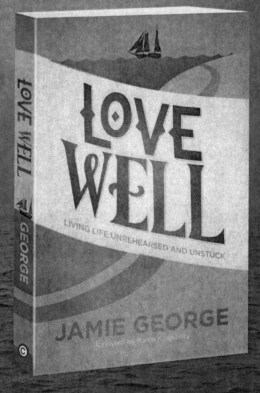
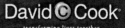

CPSIA information can be obtained at www.ICGtesting.com
Printed in the USA
LVOW07*0835220916

505711LV00004B/5/P